Wisdom With
Understanding
is Better
Than Rubies
Lurine Karon Greenberg
Fine Arts Collection

PEGGY SOMERVILLE

An English Impressionist

PEGGY SOMERVILLE

AN ENGLISH IMPRESSIONIST

STEPHEN REISS

in association with
Rosemary Somerville

ANTIQUE COLLECTORS' CLUB

ISBN 1 85149 260 7

British Library Cataloguing-in-Publication Data
A catalogue record for this book is available from the British Library

FRONTISPIECE: *Peggy, aged four, working on some new paintings.*
TITLE PAGE: ***Anemones.*** *Pencil, coloured chalks and wash on white paper. Castle Museum, Norwich.*

Printed in England by the Antique Collectors' Club Ltd.
5 Church Street, Woodbridge, Suffolk
on Consort Royal Satin paper
supplied by the Donside Paper Company, Aberdeen, Scotland

Contents

Author's note – signatures and dates on pictures

Peggy Somerville did not always sign her paintings and rarely did she date them. Nor can every inscribed date necessarily be accepted at its face value. In her early years Peggy sometimes signed Margaret Scott Somerville, Margaret S Somerville or with the initials MSS, while – at the very beginning – it was often just Peggy. Later it was generally, though not always, Peggy Somerville, or the initials PS. Often she signed on the back of the picture and, occasionally, on both back and front. There are no grounds for supposing that the fact of her signing, or how she signed, had any bearing on what she thought of the picture. Like so many artists, her approach to this aspect of her profession seems to have been entirely haphazard.

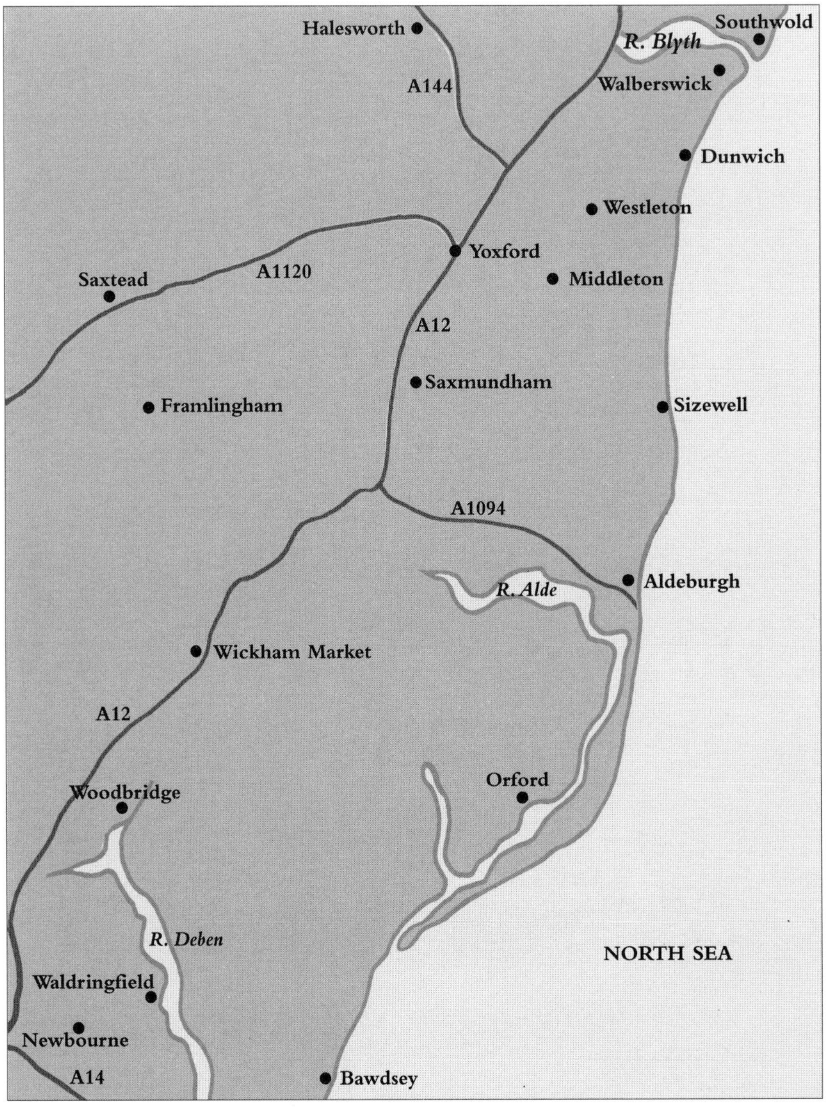

Map of East Suffolk showing the principal locations associated with Peggy.

To the memory of
Peggy Somerville
1918 – 1975

Figures in a pink landscape.
Watercolour. Aged three.

Threshing time.
Oil. Aged ten.

Antique Collectors' Club

The Antique Collectors' Club was formed in 1966 and quickly grew to a five figure membership spread throughout the world. It publishes the only independently run monthly antiques magazine, *Antique Collecting*, which caters for those collectors who are interested in widening their knowledge of antiques, both by greater awareness of quality and by discussion of the factors which influence the price that is likely to be asked. The Antique Collectors' Club pioneered the provision of information on prices for collectors and the magazine still leads in the provision of detailed articles on a variety of subjects.

It was in response to the enormous demand for information on 'what to pay' that the price guide series was introduced in 1968 with the first edition of *The Price Guide to Antique Furniture* (completely revised 1978 and 1989), a book which broke new ground by illustrating the more common types of antique furniture, the sort that collectors could buy in shops and at auctions rather than the rare museum pieces which had previously been used (and still to a large extent are used) to make up the limited amount of illustrations in books published by commercial publishers. Many other price guides have followed, all copiously illustrated, and greatly appreciated by collectors for the valuable information they contain, quite apart from prices. The Price Guide Series heralded the publication of many standard works of reference on art and antiques. *The Dictionary of British Art* (now in six volumes), *The Pictorial Dictionary of British 19th Century Furniture Design, Oak Furniture* and *Early English Clocks* were followed by many deeply researched reference works such as *The Directory of Gold and Silversmiths,* providing new information. Many of these books are now accepted as the standard work of reference on their subject.

The Antique Collectors' Club has widened its list to include books on gardens and architecture. All the Club's publications are available through bookshops world wide and a full catalogue of all these titles is available free of charge from the addresses below.

Club membership, open to all collectors, costs little. Members receive free of charge *Antique Collecting*, the Club's magazine (published ten times a year), which contains well-illustrated articles dealing with the practical aspects of collecting not normally dealt with by magazines. Prices, features of value, investment potential, fakes and forgeries are all given prominence in the magazine.

Among other facilities available to members are private buying and selling facilities, the longest list of 'For Sales' of any antiques magazine, an annual ceramics conference and the opportunity to meet other collectors at their local antique collectors' clubs. There are over eighty in Britain and more than a dozen overseas. Members may also buy the Club's publications at special pre-publication prices.

As its motto implies, the Club is an organisation designed to help collectors get the most out of their hobby: it is informal and friendly and gives enormous enjoyment to all concerned.

For Collectors — By Collectors — About Collecting

ANTIQUE COLLECTORS' CLUB
5 Church Street, Woodbridge Suffolk IP12 1DS, UK
Tel: 01394 385501 Fax: 01394 384434
or
Market Street Industrial Park Wappingers' Falls, NY 12590, USA
Tel: 914 297 0003 Fax: 914 297 0068

Colour Plates

Peggy aged three. Devon holiday, 1921.

Peggy and Rosemary aged nine and twelve.

CHAPTER I
Childhood and Adolescence

Fame came early to Margaret Scott Somerville (1918-1975), better known as Peggy. On 1st April 1922, two months before her fourth birthday, two of her recent watercolours were on view at the Thirty-third Annual Exhibition of the Royal Drawing Society at the Guildhall, London. Such was the interest they aroused that photographs of her at work appeared in the *Daily Mirror* and the *Sunday Pictorial* and she also received a mention in the *Daily Mail.* These in turn led to a flattering invitation from a prominent Bond Street photographer.

Her advance was rapid. At the age of five she was painting in oils and three years later one of her works, 'Happy Days by the Sea,' was exhibited at the New

Studio photograph of Peggy by the Bond Street photographer Swaine.

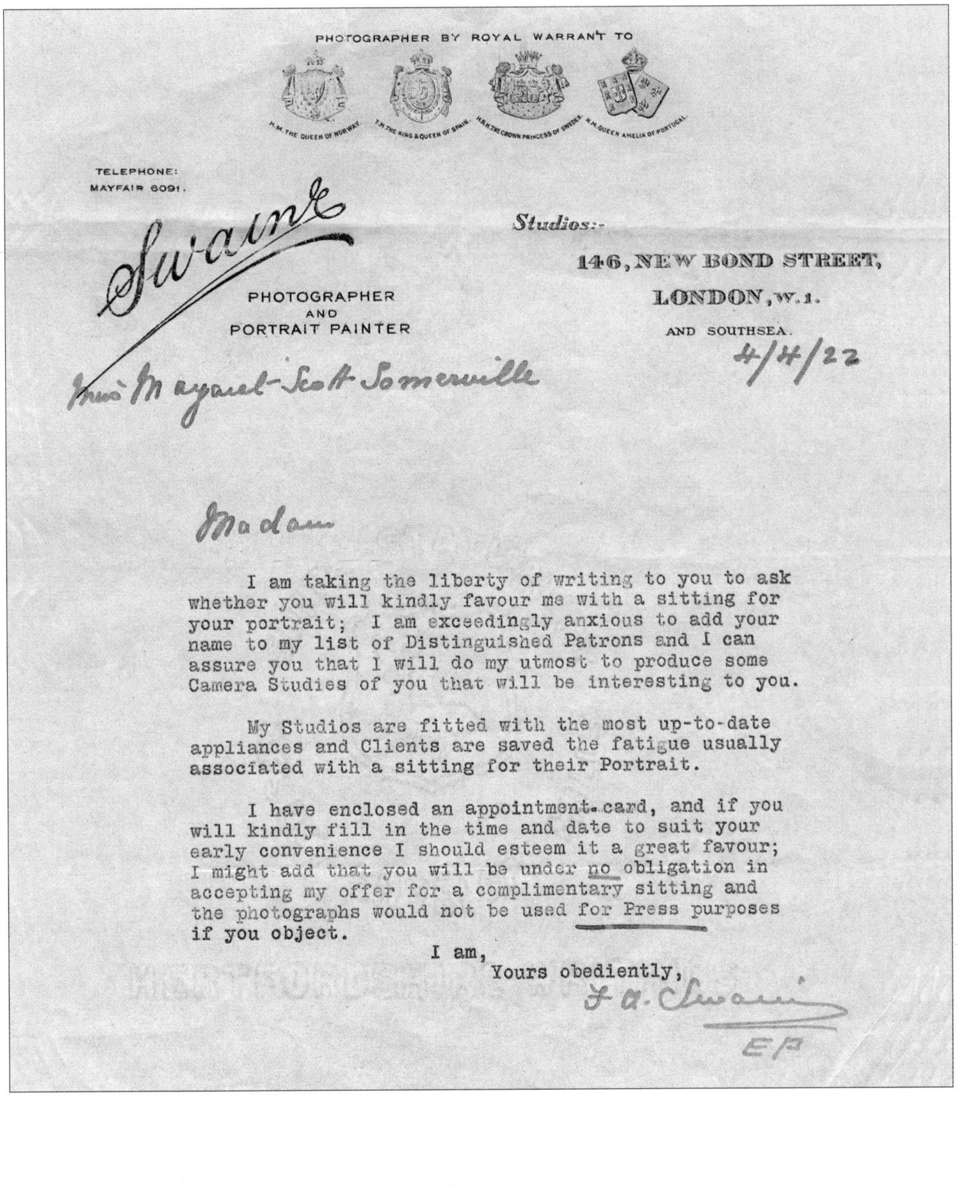

PHOTOGRAPHER BY ROYAL WARRANT TO

H.M. THE QUEEN OF NORWAY. T.M. THE KING & QUEEN OF SPAIN. H.R.H. THE CROWN PRINCESS OF SWEDEN. H.M. QUEEN AMELIA OF PORTUGAL.

TELEPHONE:
MAYFAIR 6091.

Swaine
PHOTOGRAPHER
AND
PORTRAIT PAINTER

Studios:-
146, NEW BOND STREET,
LONDON, W.1.
AND SOUTHSEA.

4/4/22

Miss Margaret Scott Somerville

Madam

I am taking the liberty of writing to you to ask whether you will kindly favour me with a sitting for your portrait; I am exceedingly anxious to add your name to my list of Distinguished Patrons and I can assure you that I will do my utmost to produce some Camera Studies of you that will be interesting to you.

My Studios are fitted with the most up-to-date appliances and Clients are saved the fatigue usually associated with a sitting for their Portrait.

I have enclosed an appointment card, and if you will kindly fill in the time and date to suit your early convenience I should esteem it a great favour; I might add that you will be under no obligation in accepting my offer for a complimentary sitting and the photographs would not be used for Press purposes if you object.

I am,
Yours obediently,
F. A. Swaine
EP

Swaine's invitation to Peggy.

WORK THAT SHOWS GENIUS

Exhibition Opened by Sir John Lavery

By Our Art Critic

To Peggy Somerville, aged 9, may be applied the words "And a little child shall lead them"—that is, the lions and the lambs of art.

Already she is painting in a way that no living artist could excel. This is not an overstatement.

Sir John Lavery, in the absence of Lady Lavery through illness, opened an exhibition of Peggy's work yesterday at the Claridge Gallery, Brook-street, W., and said he was "completely mystified by the extraordinary genius of the little girl in the handling of oils, water colours and crayons."

In support of his and one's own opinion, numerous little drawings and paintings made between the ages of three and nine could be mentioned, but, as examples, Nos. 2, 4, 5, 7, 7a, 16, 29, 34 and 42 may be noted. All are gems of great beauty, refined in sentiment and expressed with the technical assurance that comes to most artists after long experience and much vexation of spirit.

AMAZING SIMPLICITY

But mutations of atmosphere and their influence on form and colour seem to have no difficulties for Peggy Somerville. Look at the "Sun After Rain" (2). Light glimmering in the still moist air and on the landscape is suggested with amazing simplicity, and not less remarkable is the illusion of sunrise in the luminous pinks and pearly greys of No. 16.

Deeper emotion moves in "A Lonely Road" (42) and even her still-life pictures are quick with nervous vision and lovely colour.

See No. 34 and the "Ming Vase" (7), so sensitively visualised and exquisitely painted. This work was produced in a day; each of the others referred to was done in the course of a morning.

She never had a lesson. She just watched her father and brothers at work (all are artists), and became absorbed in her own.

In her third year she sent clever sketches to the Royal Drawing Society, and at the Claridge Gallery are shown other specimens of the early efforts that led up gradually to the beautiful "Ming Vase", which is her latest achievement.

In answer to a question she said, "Yes, I like music, and I dance and also read poetry." Peggy was unsophisticated enough to admit that she loved Longfellow.

There is nothing precocious about Peggy's demeanour. She is a charmingly natural child, with bright, dark eyes and fair hair, as much interested in her domestic pets as in art. It would be unwise to prophesy as to her future development. She has advanced so far already that a period of apparent repose may follow, of slow but sure preparation free from artificial forcing.

As hinted, she comes of a family of artists. Her father is an able painter, her brother, Stuart, who is twenty, has exhibited regularly at the Royal Academy since he was sixteen, and a younger brother mounted his sister's pictures and made the admirable frames which display them to the best advantage.

Reviews from the Morning Post *and the* Christian Science Monitor *following the 1928 Claridge Gallery retrospective exhibition. This was opened five days after Peggy's tenth birthday by Sir John Lavery.*

Irish Salon in Dublin, chosen solely on merit without the judges having the slightest idea as to the artist's age. Then followed a retrospective at the Claridge Gallery, Brook Street, London W1. Opened by Sir John Lavery on 7th June, five days after Peggy's tenth birthday, the event was reported throughout Britain and beyond and within a few days every picture was sold. The two reviews reproduced here from the *Morning Post* (8th June, 1928) and the Boston *Christian Science Monitor* (19th July, 1928), give a fair idea of the family background and the bewilderment felt, not only then but also since. A few questions still remain unanswered. As Whistler famously pointed out, we cannot measure the input of a work of art by the amount of time spent on it. Nor should we be deceived by the appearance of simplicity. For many artists the overriding aim is to release, not to burden. For them the essence of art is to conceal art.

So where does this leave the art of children? Peggy, who knew how to write as well as to paint, recalled her childhood work in a letter in a letter to her mother in 1952, 'Looking at mine brought back a million memories – of the Old Ford Farm – my early dreams – my joys in nature. Speaking in a detached way, as an artist, I would say some of these drawings and paintings are beautiful in their simplicity. Nothing is more pure than the first spontaneous expression of a child – its very lack of consciousness proves its closer link with God. Later there comes the conscious struggle to accept all things and still feel life as magical, as full of wonder, as one did as a child.' There is something elemental about the work of a child, like the sun on the sea, the movement of an animal, the wind in the trees. Can it therefore be accepted as art, which by its very nature is artificial?

Do we really need to know? The fact is Peggy's childhood works are so enchanting they simply cannot be dismissed. In some respects they may indeed be unique. Where else can we find such a quantity of work surviving from the age of three onwards, work which passes through several different phases, always

Exhibition
of
PAINTINGS
and
DRAWINGS
by
PEGGY SOMERVILLE
at the
CLARIDGE GALLERY,
52, BROOK STREET. W.1.

JUNE 7th—JUNE 23RD, 1928.

A Child Artist

SPECIAL FROM MONITOR BUREAU
London

PEGGY SOMERVILLE is a remarkable little girl. At three years of age she was an exhibitor at the Royal Drawing Society, and before her tenth birthday she had her own "one man" show at the Claridge Gallery. That between £300 and £400 worth of her infinitesimal oil paintings and water colors were sold during her exhibition would not surprise anyone who saw them, they were so charming, so obviously desirable. It is only when one realizes that the artist was eight or nine years old when they were done that the thing becomes a mystery.

Margaret Somerville (to give this little artist the grown-up "real" name she received from her parents) was born into a family of artists exactly 10 years ago. Her father is Charles Somerville, the distinguished portraitist and landscape painter; her 20-year-old brother has exhibited at the Royal Academy since he was 16; two other brothers and a sister also paint; what else could little Peggy do? All five, indeed, send regularly to the Royal Drawing Society's exhibitions. So, painting and drawing up to exhibition standards can be truly said to be child's play to the members of this astonishing family.

They live deep in the country, in an old farmhouse by a ford. There are no art schools near, no stultifying artists' cliques. Each works independently of the other. The child Peggy is practically untaught as yet. She teaches herself by trying over and over again. She watches her father and her big brother at work. Sometimes she can pick up valuable hints from seeing their way of doing things, though the effects she wishes to get do not appear on their canvases. She has her own ideas about what she wants to paint. No one can influence her here.

The work shown ranged from drawings done six years ago to the little oil paintings and water-color sketches of her past two years. It was possible to see, therefore, the child's rapid development in craftsmanship, and how it proceeds parallel to her gradual unfolding as an artist. The more precise her observations are and the more vivid her impressions, the greater her ease in registering them. This augurs well for her future. Usually with the child prodigy, craftsmanship lags far behind artistic sensitiveness and impressionability. (Incidentally, this is why so little is ever heard of them as adult professionals.) Peggy Somerville is learning rapidly. Already she can express most of what she sees, fluently, with only occassional awkwardnesses — as, for instance, when she experiments with horses. A horse is not an easy subject for anyone to paint or draw. This little girl is finding out little by little how it can be done.

But her excellent sense of composition is the most promising sign that her talent is real and individual, and not merely the facility for clever imitation, which children so often have. She is not content quite simply to record her observations. She has the true creative longing to make something of her own out of them. So she arranges with conscious art the groups of figures, the beggars and gypsies who have been coming to the old ford as long as she can remember, and in landscape knows instinctively how to eliminate all fluffy detail and emphasize the design by careful accenting of its main features.

Her color sense is delicately appropriate to the present diminutive size of her canvases. The little paintings have the quality of fragile porcelain ornaments in consequence. The most ambitious, dimensionally as well as artistically, is the still life entitled "The Ming Vase," a delicious flower study in pastel shades.

Animals and gypsies interest her more than other living beings just now, and she is at her best when she can introduce some such sign of life into her dainty pastorals. It is indeed a child's vision that vivifies these enchanting sketches of "Cows by a Pond," of "Gypsies at Dinner," of "Early Spring and Sheep," to name some of the most characteristic, and our own inner life is the richer for having come into contact with it.

F. R.

evolving, as though after all it had been the outcome of much deliberate thought? For the survival of this work we have her mother and father to thank. They knew Peggy was exceptional, and they were not without experience in these matters.

Peggy's father, Charles Somerville, 1870-1939.

Her father, Charles Somerville (1870-1939), was a minor player in a major movement, a movement already firmly rooted in Britain, Ireland, France, the Netherlands, Germany, Italy, Scandinavia and America; no country would be left untouched by it. In essence it was anti-academic, wedded to the open-air and the contemporary scene, high-keyed in its range of colours, and generally objective in its approach. It goes under the comprehensive banner of Impressionism, a term with many facets. At one extreme, it describes the simple life, man's exposure to nature, and at the other it represents a direct spontaneous response to any given visual experience, no matter how sophisticated. A multitude of different technical procedures lie between these two.

Charles Somerville, who besides being a painter was sometimes an art teacher, picture restorer, dealer and, in the war years, farmer, was on the rural wing of the movement. He had learnt *alla prima* from the Glasgow Boys and memory painting from Joseph Crawhall. Coming south from Scotland towards the end of the century, he would get to know many of the leading painters of the day, those

Peggy's mother, Rose Anne, before her marriage. 1905.

linked with Newlyn and Dublin, as well as Frank Brangwyn and Charles Conder. Yet the artist whose work most closely approaches his is perhaps Arthur Peppercorn, whose subdued and moody productions owed so much to Barbizon and The Hague. As there is no record of the two artists ever having met, their similarity may only reflect the prevailing artistic climate, with its greater dependence on Millet than Monet.

His first wife died in 1904 leaving him with two children. His second wife, Rose Anne or Nan as she was usually called, had travelled widely while working with the Asquith family, and she entirely shared Charles's artistic aspirations. She bore him six children and, as neither had any money behind them and Charles's earnings were small, they spent the whole of their married life in comparative poverty.

As history tells us, it is not the great painters who have produced the prodigies but the less gifted, or at least those whose gifts, for one reason or another, were never fulfilled. So it was with the Somerville family. Both Charles and Nan were determined to encourage every artistic leaning their children might possess. They should have the best their limited resources could buy, and their path was eased in every way possible. They were, for instance, offered a scullery wall on which to wipe the surplus paint off their brushes, instead of the laborious process (also harmful to the brushes) of washing them in white spirit. They must learn for themselves by observation and memory. There should be no copying either directly from nature or from the work of others. It must always be their own invention based on what they had seen, and they should avoid changing or interfering with what they had done; rather they should begin again, perhaps many times.

In May 1926, the *Daily Mirror* published a photograph of the six children. By then Forbes was nineteen, Stuart eighteen, Gordon sixteen, Kenneth fourteen, Rosemary eleven and Peggy seven. As the caption tells us, Stuart's work had already been accepted and hung in the Royal Academy. All eyes were now, however, turning towards the youngest member of the family. Everyone was agreed that, except for her painting, she was just like any other child. She loved her dolls, the family pets, playing games, climbing trees, bonfires, and watching the gypsy encampment in the

The Somerville family c.1913 near Thorne, Yorkshire before Peggy was born. The central standing figure is Nancy, daughter by Charles's first marriage.

field across the stream which bounded the Old Ford Farm. But her painting was extraordinary. At the age of six and seven Peggy had been producing pictures like 'A Gathering at Night' and 'Watching the Sea,' highly imaginative and only to a small extent based on what she had actually seen. A year later, however, her approach had changed. In common with other children from the age of seven or eight onwards, the direct visual experience became more important to her. In 'Happy Days by the Sea,' the picture her father submitted to the New Irish Salon in Dublin when

Photograph of the six Somerville children published by the Daily Mirror *in May 1926.*

The Ford, Ashford, 1918.

she was eight, she remembers a holiday in Devon and is plainly trying to be realistic. Nevertheless imagination still plays a large part and we experience an extraordinary evocation of remote antiquity, the age of the Druids. (Was it perhaps this Celtic flavour which led Charles Somerville to think of Dublin?)

By the time of the 1928 Claridge Gallery exhibition in London's Brook Street this change of approach had been carried a stage further, as can be seen for instance in 'The Lane in Spring'. The subject is still fictional, for we know that no child would have been allowed to pitch a bonfire so close to the road. At the same time how accurately she has observed the smoke drifting towards the trees, a theme which had always fascinated her and about which she wrote in a poem to her mother a few years later –

We will gather round the camp fire
Watch the blue smoke curl and fly
Watch it lingering in the tree tops
Then pass on towards the sky.

With her amazing 'Primroses', painted at the age of ten, her powers of observation had reached their apogee. And yet even here we are compelled to acknowledge that she has recreated the subject in her own mind, in terms of tone and colour. When a reporter asked her how she set about painting her pictures, she replied quite simply, 'I see the picture in my mind and then just paint it.'

The factor which most clearly distinguishes her work from that of other children is her handling. This was emphasised by Sir John Lavery when he opened Peggy's first solo exhibition at the Claridge Gallery. He confessed himself 'completely mystified by the extraordinary genius of the little girl in the handling of oils, watercolours and crayons.' It was as if she had been thrown into the water and at once knew how to swim. Nothing daunted her. No matter what she held in her hand, pen, pencil, charcoal, chalk, crayon, fat loaded brush or mean skinny

Peggy, aged eight, drawing Joan Clarkson of Cochran's Revue, reproduced in Eve, The Lady's Pictorial, *9th June 1926.*

brush, water, oil or wax, it was all the same – she knew how they wanted her to lead them and she happily accepted the challenge. It was not 'what' but 'how' she painted that enchants us.

In his review of this exhibition in the *Morning Post*, the critic Ian Colvin had advocated there should follow a period of 'slow but sure preparation free from artificial forcing.' Not surprisingly, therefore, accusing fingers were pointed at Charles Somerville and the Gallery when a second exhibition was presented in the same location only a year later. The publicity was even wider than before and prices were higher but the public did not respond with quite the same enthusiasm and Charles recognised his mistake. As for Peggy, she had hardly taken in what

Peggy, aged nine, photographed at Old Ford Farm, Ashford, Middlesex, with a painting entitled ***Cows in a meadow****, shown above.*

Nancy (Peggy's eldest sister) feeding the ducks. Oil. Charles Somerville.

had been happening and just carried on exactly as before. Her only known reaction was annoyance with the press photographers because they insisted on showing her painting out of doors, which she never did; she made drawings outside but never paintings.

The well-known art historian and critic R.H.Wilenski wrote an amusing piece in the *Evening Standard* claiming that Peggy had done a great service by proving that what he called 'pseudo-impressionism' was child's play. Of course, his whole approach was absurdly prejudiced, according to the fashion of those times, but it makes a good read nonetheless.

In October the same year (1929) Peggy submitted her painting 'The Cornfield' (page 30) to the Royal Institute of Oil Painters (the R.O.I. Wilenski so disparaged), and this was accepted and hung. After this her father acceded to widespread advice and kept Peggy under wraps until November 1932, when a further one hundred of her oil paintings were shown at the Beaux Arts Gallery in Bruton Street. The reviews were again as rapturous as they had been in 1928. That of the *Morning Post* is reprinted as well as a letter to *Country Life* by the eminent critic and art historian Mary Chamot.

Infant prodigies are not unknown in the history of the visual arts, but little of their work before the age of fourteen has survived, or is recognised as such – Raphael, Van Dyck, Paulus Potter, Elisabetta Sirani, Raphael Mengs, Morland, Lawrence, Bonington, Millais, to mention only a few. A rare exception is the Dutch artist Gerard ter Borch (1617-1681) whose father, like Charles Somerville, was careful to preserve his children's work. In their confident simplicity, this artist's childhood drawings have something in common with Peggy's. The same could be said of the early drawings of Toulouse-Lautrec, the outstanding prodigy of more recent times. It may be noted that, although child art has been widely studied in an educational context, it has never, except in the case of the present

Pen drawing by the Dutch artist, Gerard ter Borch (1617-1681), aged seven.

SPLODGING INTO ART AT 11 YEARS OF AGE.

Peggy Somerville Proves that Pseudo-Impressionism is Child's Play.

By R. H. WILENSKI.

EVERYONE should go to the exhibition of fifty landscapes in oil by Peggy Somerville, aged eleven, which is open at the Claridge Gallery from to-day, because this exhibition should deal the death-blow to a degraded form of pseudo-impressionism that abounds in adult art shows like the R.O.I. and the R.B.A. and one-man exhibitions in Bond-street.

For twenty-five years, since I first painted pseudo - impressionist landscapes myself, I have been convinced that this sort of picture is not art, but child's play, and now Peggy Somerville, who is really a child, has appeared to prove it.

Miss Peggy Somerville.

The pictures in this show are painted in the "splodgy" technique now used by some 50,000 painters in England. As far as technique goes, I have seen about 50,000,000 pictures by adults exactly like Peggy's. As far as mind goes, some of the adults sometimes contribute a little more, but in most cases the contribution in this field is also about the same.

"Vulgarised Art."

Peggy's pictures, like those of her 50,000 adult colleagues, are a shocking degradation of the original art of Constable, which has been imitated, mauled about and vulgarised by painters, all day, every day, for exactly a hundred years.

Ruskin described Constable's faculty as "blunt and untrained . . . wholly disorderly, slovenly and licentious, . . . and consummately mischievous first in its easy satisfaction of the painter's own self-complacencies and then in the pretence of ability which blinds the public to all the virtue of patience and to all the difficulty of precision."

What would he have said of Peggy Somerville and the 50,000 grown-up Peggies of to-day?"

He would have said, of course, "I told you so," because elsewhere he wrote: "You might more easily fill a house with pictures like Constables's from garret to cellar than imitate one cluster of leaves by Van Eyck or Giotto." The Peggies have now filled the houses of a whole country with their child's play; and but for the lessons taught us by the Cubists we might still be confusing their derivative concoctions with original art.

Peggy's Pictures.

Peggy herself is a frail and tiny tot. I am a short man, but she only reaches to my waist. She has golden brown hair, dark eyes and an ivory skin. Her father told me that some of her pictures have been painted in twenty minutes. At an exhibition she had at the age of nine she sold, it is stated, to the value of approximately £400. If she sells all the pictures in her present show at catalogue prices she will make about £680 (minus, I presume, the gallery's commission).

Her father has arranged for her to stay away from school on days when she feels in the mood to go out in the fields round her country home and paint.

She comes of a family of painters. Her father paints, her brother paints, her sister paints. She has been to the Tate Gallery. Somehow or other she has got her poor little child's eye so full of pseudo-Constable-impressionist pictures that she can already see nothing except in those terms. Her skill in the mixing of colours, particularly greys, and her facility in "splodging" them on canvas, are the result of a monkey-like capacity for imitating such pictures.

All intelligent artists know that when they see nature in terms of other people's pictures they are *ipso facto* incapable of a personal reaction until they have shaken themselves free of the influence. Peggy is now in this disastrous stage. She can no longer see the world with the marvellous vision of a child, which is based on curiosity (the instinct of wanting to understand). She will not be able to get any other genuine reaction till she can free her eye and mind from other people's "splodgy" pictures.

When that happens she may develop into the long-awaited first-rate woman artist. Meanwhile she has to develop from a tiny tot to a little girl, from a little girl to a flapper and from a flapper to a woman.

Great art is the record of the finest perceptions or the grandest imagination of the human mind. Peggy at eleven need not be dismayed that she cannot produce it But the 50,000 adult Peggies must see this exhibition and then go home and think.

YOUNG ARTIST'S GENIUS

Striking Work by Miss Peggy Somerville

PROMISE FULFILLED

By Our Art Critic

What is to be said about Miss Peggy Somerville and her paintings on view at the Beaux Arts Gallery, Bruton-place, Bruton-street, W. ?

Four years ago, at the age of nine, she was hailed as a genius, which was the only word one dare use when driven into an impasse by the quality of the work then exhibited by her in the Claridge Gallery.

She had no academic training, nothing but the example of her father, who practised art more or less as a hobby.

Yet her outlook on nature was so discriminating, so sure, and her technique so competent, that the query came, "Why waste large sums of money on art schools when a child who has never crossed the threshold of one can reach such a high standard alone by force of her innate talents? Is it wise to encourage any boy or girl less gifted to follow an artistic career?"

This reasoning led to a question of doubt. If given time would she develop, or was her success merely the transient expression of a volatile child? The immediate sequel seemed to answer the latter interrogation.

Within a year (I think) of her first exhibition she was allowed to hold a second but the work was so inferior that all hope of her future redemption was generally abandoned.

But fortunately that was a mistaken renunciation. The child was afterwards allowed to develop naturally and the remarkable collection at the Beaux Arts Gallery is the fruit of her parents' wisdom.

VITAL IN SPIRIT

The pictures are small in size, but vital in spirit, big in design, broad in treatment, yet subtle in the nuances of light and shade and colour. There are few false notes, rhythms are continuous, like nerves quickening every part of her landscapes.

In studying them Constable comes to mind, and the conclusion reached is that the best of these vivid impressions are as good as any of the master's finest sketches. Look, for example, particularly at Nos. 9, 18, 20, 36, 37, 39, 65, 66, 87, 92, and 106.

All her works are in low palpitating tones, deepened to old master-like harmony, to some extent through the paint having sunk into the wood panels on which apparently they are painted.

What will Miss Peggy Somerville do next? Will her art become more significant in expression? She, having once more brought us into a mental cul-de-sac, we must wait until she leads us out again.

A FOURTEEN YEAR OLD ARTIST

TO THE EDITOR OF "COUNTRY LIFE."

SIR,—May I draw your attention to the very remarkable exhibition of paintings by Peggy Somerville at the Beaux Arts Gallery? Peggy Somerville is now fourteen, and held her first exhibition at the age of nine. It is said that she has had no drawing lessons, but has learnt all she knows by watching her father, who is an amateur landscape painter. It is, of course, impossible in these days of art galleries, exhibitions and reproductions, for anyone to reach the age of fourteen and not have some acquaintance with the work of the Masters; but as this child has lived always in the country, it is obvious that she has learnt far more from nature than from art. Her approach towards landscape is a perfectly frank enjoyment of the beauty of the English countryside, and an astonishing power of reproducing what she sees in terms of paint. The surprising thing about her work is that there is nothing childish about her vision. She does not paint concepts of things, representing them in outline and flat colour, and arranging them in agreeable patterns like most children do, but paints the full complexity of the atmospheric effect, which, in the history of European painting, first appears in Constable's work. Indeed, Peggy Somerville's paintings are very like some of Constable's sketches from nature, except that she usually chooses warmer, gayer aspects of English country life. Her eye for composition is unerring, and her touch absolutely masterly. Using always the same scale, and a brown-toned painting board for her ground, she avoids some of the pitfalls which beset the landscape painter; but, even so, the assurance of her work and the amount of her output are almost incredible. In view of the fact that this obviously gifted young artist has quite naturally found the means of expression best suited to her, one is inclined to question whether art school training has any advantages. In any case, it is to be hoped that Peggy Somerville will be allowed to continue the development of her own style without the risk of having other men's vision and technique imposed upon her. She certainly has little to learn in the matter of landscape painting.—MARY CHAMOT.

A review from the Morning Post *and a letter to* Country Life *by the eminent critic and art historian Mary Chamot following Peggy's successful 1932 exhibition at the Beaux Arts Gallery.*

artist, been seen as a prelude to a lifetime devoted to producing pictures.

It could be said that Peggy's childhood career ended in September 1931, three months after her thirteenth birthday, when she, her parents and her sister Rosemary left the Old Ford Farm and moved to Shimpling, a small hamlet in the heart of Suffolk. She had finished her schooling and with two solo West End exhibitions behind her and a third on the way, she could consider herself a full-time artist. As she told a reporter, 'Thank goodness I don't have to go to school any more. Father does not agree with being stuffed up with useless knowledge. I said I did not want to go to school any more, and he just let me leave. I only care for my painting, and I love the countryside. I paint on anything I can find, and like wood and cardboard just as well as canvas.'

With the onset of adolescence, however, the early certainties began to slip. It was as if she could see a new life, a whole new world, stretching before her, and now she felt the need for more guidance. The choice logically fell on her brother Stuart (1908-1983). They had always been close but for the next ten years or so they were even closer and he became her role model.

Born in 1908, and therefore ten years older than Peggy, Stuart, artistically the most gifted of her elder brothers and sisters, had shown an exceptional aptitude both for painting flowers and making drawings in the manner of the old masters, especially Claude Lorrain. Since 1925 he had exhibited regularly at the Royal Academy. Leaving home in 1930 he had settled for a time at Ditchling in Sussex and it was here that he came under the influence of Eric Gill and his circle. His style developed into a kind of fusion between Art Nouveau (Beardsley,

The bride and groom. *Watercolour 3¼in x 6in. Aged four or five.*

A gathering at night.
Chalks. 6½in x 7½in.
Aged five or six.

Brangwyn, Augustus John, Conder) and Art Deco. In those days few artists could make their living solely by painting and for the vast majority it was necessary to teach or find some commercial side-line. Stuart was no exception, more especially as it was his ambition to help his hard-pressed parents and for a time, therefore, he moved into wallpaper design, book jackets, and posters.

Happy days by the sea. *Oil on board. 5in x 6in. Aged eight. The picture exhibited at the New Irish Salon in Dublin. Castle Museum, Norwich.*

During these years (1933-36) Peggy was happy to go along with much of this,

Watching the sea. *Chalks. 3½in x 5½in. Aged seven.*

Shimplingthorne Hall. *Pencil drawing by Charles Somerville, 1933. He rented the house 1931-1934.*

and even her gypsies began to assume a voluptuous appearance and sport long flowing robes. She was not, however, a decorator, and never would be. Light, air and space had come to mean too much to her and she continued to devote herself almost exclusively to outdoor scenes. On the personal level the Stuart relationship also meant much to Peggy and in due course he introduced her to his friends where her vivacity quickly made her a welcome addition to his circle. As it happens, however, it was not through Stuart but through their half sister Nancy that Peggy met the man who mattered most to her throughout the 1930s and early 1940s.

Charles Kouveld and Rodolfa Lhombino, wedding photograph 1910.

Nancy (1895-1976), the only surviving child of Charles's first marriage, had long remained at home with the family, helping in all that was needed, much loved by everyone. By the late 1920s, however, her presence ceased to be crucial and she took a job with the Kouvelds. Charles Kouveld (1889-1963) was half Dutch and had reached a high position in the Shell Oil Company. He had married a well-known Norwegian singer, Rodolfa Lhombino (1881-1971), whose mother had been a protégé of Edvard Grieg and who herself had been one of the three girls on the bridge in Munch's famous lithograph. As Rodolfa was now running a singing school based at the Wigmore Hall, Nancy's duties were largely administrative. With no children of their own, the Kouvelds went some way towards adopting Rosemary and Peggy, often inviting them to stay at their house in central London; and so came about the romantic relationship Kouveld–Peggy. What began as a schoolgirl fantasy developed into a deep commitment, not only for Peggy but also for Charles Kouveld. His aim was to promote Peggy's career and her's was to paint in a way which would please him. It was with his help that she spent six months in Holland in 1936, staying first with the Bensincks near Middleburg and later with the Kaasjagers in Flushing (Vlissingen), both on Walcheren Island. For part of the time she was joined by Rosemary, who had visited the Bensinks two years earlier. Peggy painted and

Gathering in a Mediterranean city. *Pencil drawing by Stuart Somerville. 5in x 4in. Mid 1920s.*

Woodland idyll. *Pencil drawing by Peggy Somerville. 6in x 4in. Mid 1930s.*

Girl drying herself.
c.1935. Black chalk. 7in x 4in. A drawing of Peggy's adolescence.

The lane in spring. *Aged nine. Oil on board. 7½in x 9in.*

drew a great deal and the material she collected, together with her memories, supplied her with subjects for several years. In some ways her work advanced, for instance she succeeded in mastering tone values without sacrificing the freshness of her brushwork. On the other hand, we may regret the partial disappearance of those intuitive, mercurial characteristics of her childhood pictures, that magic she was so miraculously able to recapture in her later years.

Kouveld was something of a pedant in artistic matters. For instance in 1937, in the midst of high praise, he had the temerity to suggest 'a better fusing of the colours . . . some of which don't blend.' He wanted to sell her pictures to his City friends but was obliged to recognise the boldness of her style was too strong for them. It was largely through his influence also that Peggy was persuaded to enter the Royal Academy Schools, a step her father had always deprecated. However, the episode was short-lived as the year was 1939. Due to her father's death in May of that year, her entry was delayed three weeks and then, with the outbreak of war in August, she did not return in September.

Her father had not been well for some time and this, together with financial difficulties, had led to several changes of location. In 1934 he, Nan and Peggy had

Primroses. *Oil on board. 12in x 10in. Aged ten.*

Peggy with Charles Kouveld, 1937.

Peggy in Holland, August 1936.

Peggy with Charles Kouveld, 1937.

moved from Shimpling to nearby Cavendish and late in 1936 they settled in Wiggington near Tring. It was here that her father died and here too that Peggy and her mother stayed throughout the war years.

Looking back at the 1930s, the years of Peggy's adolescence, we can see that to some extent she had lost her way. In her haste to achieve maturity she had gone too far too soon and she had, moreover, equated adulthood with a world inhabited by men. Striving to speak their language she had invested her work with a relatively male character which, as never before or since, is recognisable as Somerville but not always as Peggy. She produced, however, many fine paintings during these years, among them 'Winter, Holland,' in which we marvel at her virtuosity in drawing trees, windmills and distant fields with single strokes of the brush. The sensitive interplay of warm and cool tones and the subtle interlocking of the planes are also to be admired. Indeed, such a work is in keeping with Jongkind and Daubigny and the best of the Hague School, whom half-

Mother, Kenneth, Nancy, Peggy and Rosemary at Shimpling, 1932.

Nancy, Rosemary, mother, friend, father and Peggy outside Fox House, Wiggington, near Tring. July 1937.

Cavendish, Suffolk. Where Peggy and her parents were living 1934-1936.

consciously she was seeking to emulate. It is a tribute to her versatility that some of her admirers might prefer the work of this period of her life to all others. Uncharacteristic, however, it still remains.

The war years were spent with Peggy living alone with her mother at Fox House, Wiggington. She took a job on the land and this was confirmed when, in 1942, she was officially called up and enrolled in the Women's Land Army. Never strong she found the work exhausting, but was grateful to remain in her beloved

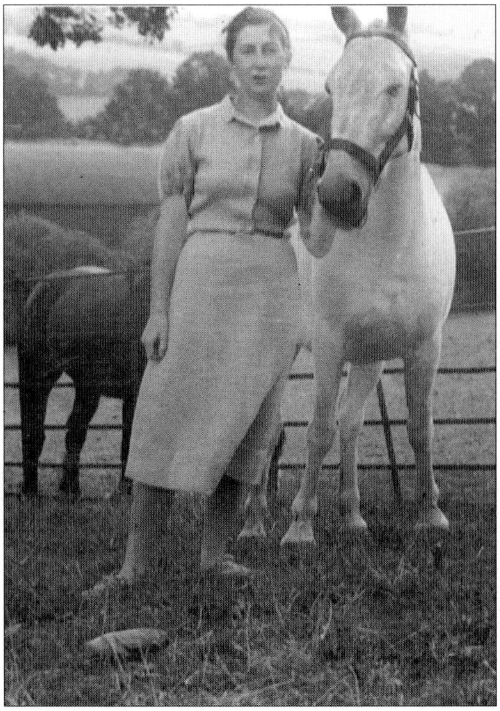

Early war years when Peggy was working on the land near Tring.

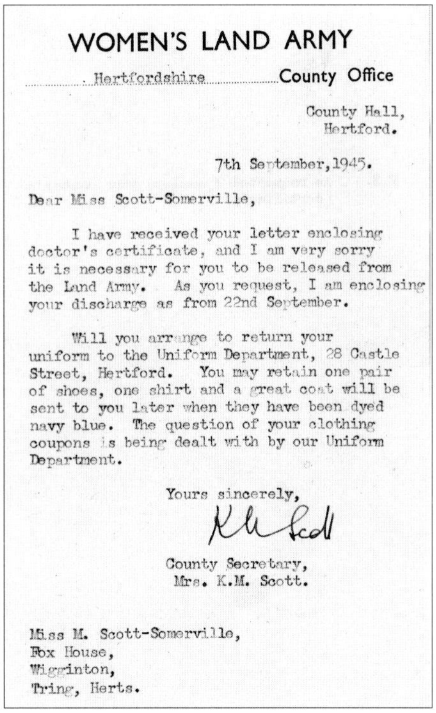

WOMEN'S LAND ARMY

Hertfordshire County Office

County Hall,
Hertford.

7th September, 1945.

Dear Miss Scott-Somerville,

I have received your letter enclosing doctor's certificate, and I am very sorry it is necessary for you to be released from the Land Army. As you request, I am enclosing your discharge as from 22nd September.

Will you arrange to return your uniform to the Uniform Department, 28 Castle Street, Hertford. You may retain one pair of shoes, one shirt and a great coat will be sent to you later when they have been dyed navy blue. The question of your clothing coupons is being dealt with by our Uniform Department.

Yours sincerely,

K M Scott

County Secretary,
Mrs. K.M. Scott.

Miss M. Scott-Somerville,
Fox House,
Wigginton,
Tring, Herts.

Letter notifying Peggy of her discharge from the Women's Land Army.

The cornfield. *Oil on board. 10in x 12in. Aged ten. Exhibited at The Royal Institute of Painters in Oil (R.O.I.) in 1929.*

countryside. Too tired at the end of each day to consider painting, her output during these years consisted of only small watercolours, usually designed as Christmas cards, in which she reverted to an earlier, prettier style. Although she and her mother were alone in the house near Tring, they received many visitors, especially the family. Juliet Laden, a friend of Peggy's whom she met at the R.A. Schools, recalls that Peggy and her mother 'were quite poor' and how 'Mrs S. made lovely meals out of practically nothing.'

At first the war brought a heightened sense of drama. Stuart, who was not yet married, declared that if he were to die he wanted everything he possessed to go to Peggy. As for Peggy, her notebooks were filled with verses about Kouveld: 'to lose you would be to lose my own soul . . . may God spare us both the loss of the other . . .' They were not intended for publication, nor even, one suspects, were they seen by Kouveld. As the war dragged on, however, Peggy gradually began to realise this romance had largely been a schoolgirl fantasy, fostered no doubt by *The Constant Nymph,* compulsive reading by all young ladies in the 1930s.

Fortunately Kouveld, despite being seriously smitten, had behaved honourably

Morning gossip. *Oil on board. 10in x 12in. Aged twelve or thirteen.*

and, when the moment of truth eventually arrived, he was warm and understanding. The two would always remain the closest of friends. Possibly it was wrong of him ever to have allowed the relationship to develop as far as it did, thereby inhibiting Peggy from forming relationships with men of her own age. Yet it must be admitted that there seems to have been something inexorable about Peggy's preference for the older man. She and Rosemary would often speak about it.

Inevitably there were a few sad casualties on the other side of the fence like Ad Kaasjager, in whose house she had stayed in 1936 and who was a young officer in the Dutch Navy. His boat had escaped the Germans and he turned up at Wiggington in 1940. 'He has loved me ever since I met him nearly four years ago,' she wrote to Stuart. 'He thought he was too young and had nothing to offer. There are all kinds of problems and love is the biggest I think.' This was one of the many things Peggy pondered during these interminable war years, years which were disastrous for many would-be artists but which for Peggy may even have been something of a blessing. She had travelled so far and so fast that a time

Ad (Adrianus) Kaasjager, a Dutch friend.

Fishermen on the quay, Flushing. *1936. Ink drawing. 11½in x 9in.*

for reflection had become almost a necessity.

The moment for which she had so long been waiting came on September 22nd, 1945. She was discharged from the Land Army and could return to her beloved painting. In the previous winter, 1944/45, to get herself in the mood, she had entered some of her Dutch pictures for two exhibitions (two at the R.O.I. and two at the R.B.A.) which had been accepted and well reviewed. But they were old pictures and her great longing was to pick up her brushes and start again with eyes refreshed by years of sleep.

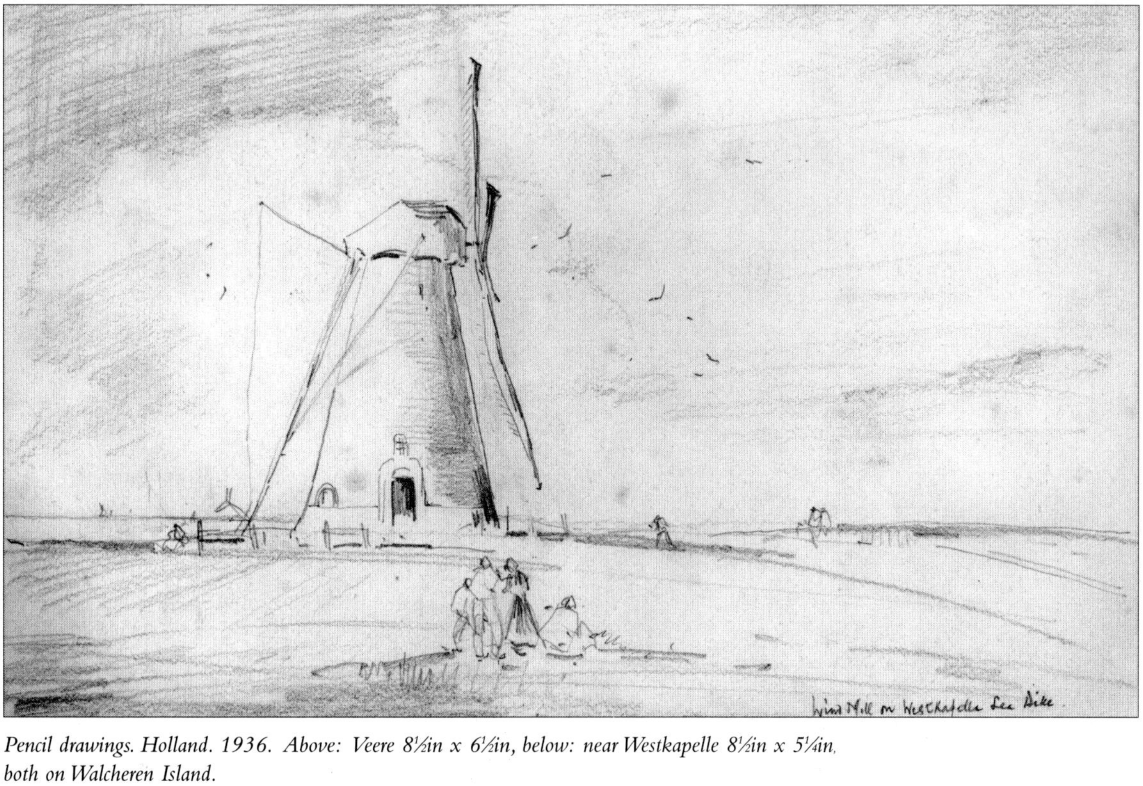

Pencil drawings. Holland. 1936. Above: Veere 8½in x 6½in, below: near Westkapelle 8½in x 5¼in, both on Walcheren Island.

Winter, Holland. *1936. Oil on board. 10in x 12in.*

Two small watercolours of Dutch views, painted by Peggy in 1936.

Two small watercolours of Dutch views, painted by Peggy in 1936.

1

2

3

4

1. Peggy with Harry Morton Colvile and her brother Stuart near Sherborne, Dorset 1938. 2. Harry with Peggy and Nancy, near Sherborne, 1938. 3. Harry with his daughter Georgiana and Pilou, 1946 and 4. Harry. c.1948.

CHAPTER II
Newbourne

In the autumn of 1945, following her release from the Land Army, Peggy and her mother left Tring and joined Stuart, his wife Catherine and their two children at Newbourne Hall, a large dilapidated Tudor mansion on the peninsula which lies between the Rivers Orwell and Deben in East Suffolk. Again, it was a new beginning, perhaps the most momentous of her life, for not only did she return to her painting from which she had so long been separated, she also found the friend who would give her the encouragement she so vitally needed. She had met him some years before and he had actually proposed to her but her commitment to Charles Kouveld had then held her back. He, Harry Morton Colvile, was Stuart's closest friend and, when Peggy and her mother arrived at Newbourne, it so happened he was helping her brother get the Hall into habitable condition. Thirteen years older than Peggy, he too was a painter. Although he had married Geraldine FitzGibbon only three years before, this did not prevent his renewed interest in Peggy. This time she found Harry's advances impossible to resist. Handsome, supremely self-assured, with a wicked sense of humour, aristocratic, and widely knowledgeable on all matters artistic, he had no difficulty in persuading Peggy he was, or would be, a substantial artist. 'I am convinced of your utter sincerity . . . you will do great things,' she wrote in May 1946.

But there were problems. It was only too obvious that Harry's affection for Geraldine was by no means over, let alone his adoration for their little daughter Georgiana. That Peggy could ever be a marriage wrecker, or stand between a father and his child, would strike at the very root of everything in which she

Peggy and Harry sketching near Newbourne. Note that she is only drawing. Photograph Charles Law.

Portrait of Peggy by Harry Morton Colvile. Oil on board. Painted about 1950 in a style influenced by Peggy. Photograph by Julia Davey.

believed. She herself longed for the time when she would be married and have children. By March 1946 therefore she was already writing, 'It is all too clear I must try to forget you, yet I know I shall always miss you' and on the back of one of her watercolours we find:

I stand and gaze from my attic window
Onto the wide fair fields
And though I am free to come and go as I please
I am imprisoned within myself

Despair is my constant companion
I am ashamed
I have been blessed with joy for a short time
Even as the tender play of light and shade in grass and trees
Lasts only while the sun shines

In the garden at Newbourne. *Winter 1946/7. Mary discusses a problem with Peggy's brother Stuart, Catherine carries Anne to the summer house. Oil on canvas. 12¼in x 14in.*

Yet she did not forget Harry and never would. He had only to return to Newbourne and again the sun would shine. For her it had been 'a precious awakening which nothing can touch or take away.' But what of Harry? He had married and separated before he had even met Peggy or Geraldine and was generally considered a libertine. On the other hand he was serious about Peggy. For a start he admired her enormously as an artist and this did matter to him, as indeed it did to Peggy. Moreover, he would always remain faithful to her, faithful in the sense of maintaining a solid correspondence and showering her with presents. It is true also that he began to feel he had wronged her, though Peggy herself would have none of this and always protested her gratitude – 'You have given me such happiness after years of torment and it is an intense relief to escape from that.' Harry was a curious mixture, full of contradictions. He was proud of his membership of the British landed gentry, going back to the twelfth century, yet he preferred France and the French. He was at once egotistical and generous, arrogant and humble. On his own admission he was full of prejudices; he could

Summer by the Deben.
1950. Oil on panel.
16½in x 28½in.

After the bath.
Pastel. 15in x 10in.
Early 1950s.

The Embrace. *c.1950. Black chalk. 11in x 9in. A frank statement of the relationship between Harry and Peggy.*

be cruel and yet the ground he lost was generally recovered by his particular brand of charm. *Persevere* was the family motto and Harry certainly lived up to that. He had ample private means but worked at his painting as though his life depended on it. He understood the art marvellously well, and it is therefore sad, one could say poignant, that so much input yielded so little return. As he wrote to Peggy in 1962, 'I am delighted you have sold five pictures. I do not think this ever happened to me.'

It would not be surprising if all this turmoil had retarded Peggy's return to painting. In fact, however, her painting sustained her and flourished during these early Newbourne years. There was nothing to hold her back. She had her little studio on the top floor, and she was away, painting with all the zest that was in her. The subjects she loved were all around her, the beaches, the creeks, the boating parties, the farm buildings and domestic animals, the undulating countryside, gardens, trees, flowers, children and not forgetting the fish. Nor did she lack the means to help her produce attractive, Renoir-like, nude studies (opposite). 'It is good to work here,' she wrote in 1948, 'I am full of desire to paint these days.'

Newbourne Church in winter. *c.1947. Oil on canvas. 29½in x 17½in. As seen from Peggy's attic studio in Newbourne Hall. Photograph by Julia Davey.*

She primarily worked in oils at this stage in her career, and her style was full-bodied, uninhibited, *plein air* rather than impressionist and, in its colouring, fresh, strong and warm. Her landscapes, which predominate, recall Daubigny, the early Renoir and more especially Constable (in his lighter vein), Thomas Churchyard (a particular Newbourne favourite) and Wilson Steer. Harry had been trained in France, in the school of André Lhote, and his influence certainly helped Peggy to return to the more colourful palette of her childhood days. Although her paintings were invariably composed back at the studio, they still retained the character of mint-fresh spontaneous sketches. This above all was her trade mark.

Peggy with Pat Law (later Collyns) at the 1951 Beaux Arts exhibition. Photo by Charles Law.

By 1951 Peggy had collected enough work for Frederick Lessore to be able to offer her a second solo exhibition at his Beaux Arts Gallery in Bruton Street, the first having been in 1932 when she was fourteen. The foreword spoke of her 'fine sense of composition, of tone values and of harmonious colour: her pastoral scenes, seascapes and flower-pieces are conceived and set down with the assurance of a master.' The exhibition comprised forty-three oil paintings, two pastels and one watercolour, and opened in September.

It is possible to reconstruct the contents of this exhibition, together with a few other known pre-1951 works, so as to be able to gain a very fair idea of what her early Newbourne style was like. Although landscape dominated, it covered a wide variety, including the beach, the sea, river scenes, farming scenes, farm buildings, orchards and gardens. Most contain figures, though often only one. Fruit and flowers comprise the next largest category. As one would expect, Peggy as a colourist loved flowers. As she wrote to her mother shortly before the exhibition, 'It is trying working against time . . . I have just done one of sweet williams, flowers I adore, flowers that stole my heart as a child. I can just live again moments at Ashford looking into their sweet upturned faces: I remember they grew near the gate into the orchard. This heavenly bunch came from the Watkins garden

Ballerina. *c.1950. Pastel. 11in x 14¾in. A characteristic pastel sketch of this period*

Bowls of fruit on a ledge. *Mid 1950s. Oil on panel. 9½in x 13in. The mobility of Peggy's handling was always extraordinary.*

Charlotte in the orchard. *1951. Oil on board. 12in x 10in. Charlotte was Peggy's niece and godchild.*

which is now at its best. They all come to tea on Friday. I must try and get up there today for some more flowers.' Sadly the painting 'Sweet Williams,'which was number twenty-one in the exhibition and measured 20in x 13½in. is one of the pictures it has not proved possible to trace. It is in her landscapes, however, that an East Anglian character can especially be seen, and not only because of the subject-matter. In several of these early Newbourne period pictures she recalls Constable's words – 'the sky is the key note . . . the chief organ of sentiment.' Yet the similarities are intuitive, coincidental.

The response to the 1951 Exhibition was only passable. For instance, *The Times* spoke of 'her pretty gift of soft colour in which the themes are loosely and rather mistily rendered' adding, 'but her forms seem sometimes not fully enough realised.' At once this tells us just how far the art world at this date had swung towards the more formal Post-Impressionist doctrines and Cubism in particular. Put simply, her style looked old-fashioned, *déja vu* and so it was to remain for the next thirty years. However, Peggy was not discouraged. It was Harry's belief in her that mattered most and she was delighted that one of the buyers was

Summer landscape, cornfields. *Late 1940s. Oil on canvas. 10in x 13in. The lightly undulating landscape between the Orwell and the Deben.*

Matthew Smith, a friend of Harry's.

In December 1953 Harry wrote an extended piece about Peggy's work (it is not quite clear what for). After discussing her childhood, he then continued – 'In spite of every material difficulty, in spite of the long war years in the land army and of so much time wasted against her will, Peggy Somerville is beginning now to give her measure. In this our age of originality-at-all-cost it is infinitely refreshing and gratifying to behold a completely genuine artist, almost purely instinctive, yet with a depth of feeling and a mysterious power to express it . . . Peggy Somerville never paints from nature. She makes charcoal sketches – very fine ones – and then in her studio re-creates her own world. It is to be deplored that such an artist should be hampered by circumstances and should not be able to paint more than an hour a day. Indeed it is hardly credible that under such circumstances she should manage to paint such beautiful pictures.'

It is true that conditions were tough at Newbourne, the financial stringency, the large difficult-to-manage house, the looking after mother and the children whose number had been increasing: Charlotte 1948, John 1950 and Pauline 1951. But nobody was failing to contribute. Thus Peggy would write, 'Catherine is tackling the spring cleaning with ambition, consequently I feel obliged to help, as she will kill herself otherwise.' What Harry seemed not to realise was the extent to which his intervention was hurting Peggy, who was devoted to her sister-in-law. His proposal – that Stuart and Catherine should have restricted their family for the sake of Peggy's art – was little short of monstrous.

In their attitude to children Harry and Peggy were in fact poles apart. He belonged to the 'seen and not heard' brigade. In a letter to Peggy some years later he wrote, 'I am fond of nice young things who move gracefully and are neat in every respect, but G's choice of school mates is a poor one.' In another he wrote, 'If the new generation have any sense at all, they will never have any children.'

Fen Lane, Newbourne. *Early 1950s. Oil on board. 16in x 20in.*

Fruits in the Window. *1951. Oil on board. 13in x 16in.*

Near Walberswick. *Oil on canvas. 24in x 40in. At 60 guineas, the highest priced picture in the 1951 Beaux Arts exhibition.*

The Washbrook Trout. *Signed and dated 1951. Oil on board. 14in x 16in. In a letter to her mother Peggy tells of the excitement when Stuart landed this trout by the old mill at Washbrook, near Ipswich, how the miller's wife brought out the scales (it weighed 2 lb.), and how she painted it as soon as they reached home – 'so you shall see it' – she writes.*

Peggy with Stuart and Catherine. Also Mary, Charlotte, John and Pauline. 1952. Photograph by Charles Law.

As for Peggy, however, she made no bones about the fact that, if the choice lay between marrying and having children or being a painter, she would have chosen the former and this was not being disloyal to her painting. Rather they were two great peaks which she did not think were necessarily mutually exclusive. 'It was such a heavenly morning, the birds singing, so fresh, so lovely, and I could not help wishing it were me lying up there with a little baby lying beside me.' And again, 'Little John, a sweet part of Spring. I love that child.' And, of course, we know from the way she painted children how much she loved them. For her life and art enriched each other whereas Harry seemed to see art as something separate, to be put on a pedestal.

The strain of it all began to tell on Peggy. Harry's visits to Newbourne were becoming less frequent and gradually he was establishing himself in the south of France where he had been doing up a derelict country house acquired before the war. Finally, by the end of 1953, it became clear that he, Geraldine and Georgiana were firmly settled there and for the first, and in fact only, time in her life, Peggy suffered something of a breakdown – 'It is simply that there are moments in one's life, and this is such a moment in mine, when there is a climax of years of

At the fair. *Both pictures depict three girls at a fair in Aldeburgh, c.1958. Pastel. 14in x 11in. and black chalk 9in x 6in. Peggy filled a great many sketchbooks with her drawings and then developed the most promising into her repertoire of pictures.*

self control and unuttered grief. I need a lot of strength to get me through and there are moments when I wonder if I can do it. It is not easy to live without joy – at least it has done me harm, who was born with so much capacity for enjoyment. I have tried to turn my feelings to my work, but here again it is not enough – a complete human being needs a complete life – then by being shared even the hardships and struggles can be overcome. I have tried to accept my fate and find serenity but I believe I have failed. I wanted so much to live, to give joy and happiness to others, to perhaps paint something good – but grief is killing me.'

Although this did not go to Harry, to whom she wrote only that she was unwell, the family knew and were much concerned. Because of its associations and the charged atmosphere, Peggy decided for the time being she must leave Newbourne and for the next few months she stayed at the home of her brother Forbes and his family at World's End Farm, Saxtead near Framlingham. There, in the farming environment of her childhood, she found peace and gradually her high spirits returned. Apart from a brief hiatus in the flow of pictures, this depression had no recognisable effect on Peggy's painting. Self-pity was an indulgence she despised in art as well as life and she would never permit herself for a moment to impose her private tribulations on an unsuspecting public. Not that the artistic mood should necessarily be optimistic, but feelings must be distilled and translated into an objective, universal language, and, as her brief outburst tells us, she was not the right person to give shape to the forces of darkness. Nonetheless her style was changing. There are fewer set pieces, more

Farm buildings. *Oil on board. 12in x 10in. In the 1950s Peggy's brother Forbes had a farm called World's End, near Framlingham. Some of the outbuildings are shown here.*

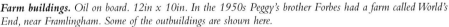

Susan, Lizzy and Jenny, her brother Forbes's three daughters. Pembroke coast.

quick sketches; her handling was becoming freer and her colouring higher keyed. Partly through Harry the French influence was more in evidence, especially Matisse and those of the Fauves' persuasion, not least Harry's friend Matthew Smith. It is sometimes claimed that Peggy was a frequent visitor to France, but this is incorrect. Apart from a two month stay in 1947, which made little impression on her style, she did not return until 1964 and would only make two further short visits, in 1966 and 1971. The fact is that, like its wine, French painting was everywhere and Peggy was among the many who imbibed it deeply.

Sensing that she needed to find new incentives, new pastures, she began to detach herself from the Deben landscape, which for the past eight years had held her in its all but exclusive thrall. Holidays with the Forbes family took her to Wales and the Pembroke coast, which she adored. An eccentric commission by a

Deckchair. *Pembroke coast, 1955. Oil on canvas. 11in x 14in. On the beach at Amroth, Pembrokeshire, where Peggy was holidaying with her brother Forbes and his family.*

Jenny and Lizzy. *Pastel. 7in x 11in. Two of Forbes's daughters, collecting seaweed from a rockpool on the Pembroke coast.*

Lockington Hall, the home of John Curzon and his model railway.

member of the Curzon family introduced her to Derbyshire and Scotland and, of most enduring significance, she became acquainted with Aldeburgh further up the Suffolk coast.

John Curzon was a model railway enthusiast and he planned an extensive network in the spacious cellars of Lockington Hall, his seat in Derbyshire. Some three rooms were involved and John invited Peggy to paint the background scenery which should relate not only to the landscape in the vicinity of Lockington Hall but also to that in the neighbourhood of his hunting lodge on Rannoch Moor, Perthshire. The work occupied Peggy intermittently over a period of three years, from mid-1956 to mid-1959. She lived in the lap of luxury while she was there, was well paid, and made some valuable contacts. Although

Shooting party on Rannoch Moor. John Curzon left, Peggy central. c.1957.

The Meet*, a pencil sketch made by Peggy while she was staying at Lockington Hall.*

she knew very well that mural painting was not her true *métier,* she made an excellent job of it by all accounts (sadly the Hall has since been converted into offices and nothing of her work has survived apart from a few sketches) – and the compensations were too good to be missed. As she wrote to her mother at about the half-way stage, 'It goes well and I must say it is worthwhile when everyone says it looks wonderful! I don't particularly *like* doing it, but it teaches me a lot and after all money is an evil necessity.' Despite her enjoyment of the luxurious living and of the many beautiful things all around her, there was also a certain unease, even foreboding, an awareness of how the neighbouring Black Country was conveniently shut off, how 'they all cry out about communism and yet they are the very people who make it.' After a particularly riotous party one evening she foresaw that 'this whirlpool of froth must suddenly be swept aside.' She supposed she was 'a socialist at heart,' and then decided 'no, a radical liberal,' and she hoped 'riches will never turn me away from the real things of life *however* difficult.' She noted, 'How strange it is that these people can possess things and yet

The so-called frontier town Port Lochinvar. Preliminary pencil drawing, background scenery to the model railway network in the cellars at Lockington Hall.

Leda and the swan.
Charcoal and watercolour. 8in x 10in. A favourite subject in the 1950s.

Below, ***Leda.***
Sepia drawing. 10½in x 7in. A study for another version of 'Leda and the swan.'

Below right,
The fair at Aldeburgh.
1957. Pastel. 14½in x 11in. The Castle Museum, Norwich.

Red boat, the Deben. *1956. Oil on board. 8in x 10in. Compare page 40,* ***Summer by the Deben.*** *Peggy often made later versions of favoured compositions.*

Breakfast table. *1959. Pastel. 13½in x 11in. Shows the influence of Anne Redpath.*

Child on horseback.
Late 1950s. Sepia drawing. 9in x 5½in. See also page 96 for a pastel on the same subject.

not *have* them, while I, poverty-stricken, hold them in my heart forever.' Politics interested her, though only spasmodically. Kouveld had tended to be on the left whereas Harry was an arch-Conservative. As an ardent Christian and church-goer, she was saddened by 'the falsity of the clergy's position as privileged officers of what is, in appearance at any rate, a small mostly middle-class body of partisan people,' and she was convinced this image must change if the church was ever to regain the confidence and respect of the whole population.

Peggy, July 1957.

Meanwhile, she had come fully to accept the limitations of her relationship with Harry and this was reinforced by a chance meeting at Lockington Hall in February 1957. Among the many visitors was 'a delightful elderly couple, Count and Countess Poklewski. She is Russian and was maid-in-waiting to the Tzarina – she is the most amazing woman in a brilliant witty way. He is a Pole, charming and intelligent, with a wealth of knowledge, and also that rare gift of enjoying nature to the full. Everyone soon called us soul mates.' A deep friendship grew between the three of them and the Poklewskis invited Peggy to visit them at their cottage on the Duchess of Kent's estate at Iver. Until his sudden death in November 1962 aged seventy-one, Alik eclipsed Harry in Peggy's most intimate affections. This only served to strengthen the bonds between Peggy and Zoia, who was later to write, 'He loved you so much and always enjoyed his times with you.' It had been an oasis in an otherwise rather barren period, and Peggy's spirits had been greatly lifted because of it.

Alik Poklewski.

Promenade, Aldeburgh. *c.1960. Signed vertically at the side of the pram. Pastel. 11in x 7¼in. The stylish mother (or nanny) approaches the south end of the Crag Path, Aldeburgh.*

CHAPTER III
Westleton & Middleton

In 1960 Peggy and her mother left Newbourne. With the growing family (another child was on the way) there was scarcely still room for them and besides there was a mutual feeling that the joint enterprise had somehow outlived its usefulness, that more could now be given and received through independence. Nonetheless, it was a tough time what with the looking for somewhere to live, the setting up of a new home and the looking after Nan who was now almost blind. The additional effort of both producing pictures and marketing them proved almost too much. She came to depend increasingly on selling locally and virtually severed all links with the London art world. 'A hateful job' was how she described the business of carting her pictures round the London galleries.

It was in the area of Aldeburgh, some eighteen miles further north, that Peggy decided to look. It had several attractions for her. Aldeburgh itself had become a

Peggy. *c.1960. Pastel. 22in x 15in. Castle Museum, Norwich.*

Conversation. *Peggy's mother with John, her grandson. c.1960. Pastel. 15in x 11in.*

Hill House, Westleton where Peggy and her mother lived 1960-64.

major arts centre, mainly through its annual festival, and Peggy had come to know it well through staying with her friend Juliet Laden, whose home was on the sea front. It also formed a triangle with the homes of her two brothers, Forbes and Stuart, at Saxtead and Newbourne. At first Peggy and her mother rented a house in Westleton and then in 1964, with borrowed money, Peggy acquired the Stone House at Middleton. It was here that they both remained until Nan died in 1971 and Peggy in 1975. From the very beginning Peggy was deeply attached to the

The Stone House, Middleton. Peggy's home from 1964 until she died in 1975.

The Stone House orchard showing the outhouse which became Peggy's studio.

Stone House and its garden. It had not been modernised and was difficult to manage but somehow she coped.

During the period of these moves Harry proved a tower of strength. He believed passionately in Peggy's unique artistic gifts and was increasingly concerned as to how he had behaved towards her. He gave her whatever money he could scrape together and lent her furniture and silver – 'Please show me that you trust me as your true friend and do not hesitate to make use of me.' Painting was the great bond between them and it was exclusively on this that their thoughts were now concentrated. Their gods were the same and they loved to converse about them: Matisse, Derain, Bonnard, Vuillard, Modigliani, Renoir, Cézanne and, further back, Delacroix, Géricault, Goya, Rembrandt and many others. Harry was an authority on Cézanne and wrote and lectured marvellously well about him, though for Peggy he was not an especial favourite. They both had reservations about Picasso, seeing him more as a draughtsman than a painter and believing it folly to attempt to learn from him.

In one of her notebooks Peggy recorded an attributed statement reported in the *Daily Telegraph* on 30th August 1960: 'From the moment art ceases to be the food that feeds the best minds, the artist can use his talents to perform all the tricks of an intellectual charlatan. The refined, the rich, the professional do-nothings, the distillers of quintessence, desire only the peculiar, the sensational, the eccentric, the scandalous in today's art. And I myself, since the advent of cubism, have fed these fellows what they wanted and satisfied the critics with all the ridiculous ideas that have passed through my head.' Although the authenticity of this has been questioned, the fact remains that it is precisely what Peggy and Harry thought Picasso ought to have said.

As for Peggy's own painting, this was continuing to change and develop. For one thing she was switching increasingly from oils to pastel, so much so that by April 1962 Harry was already asking her whether she had given up oils completely. Although she denied this, pastels were certainly Peggy's most favoured

Interior, Hill House, Westleton. *A friend visiting Peggy's mother who is in bed. Early 1960s. Pastel. 14in x 10½in.*

South Look-out, Aldeburgh. *c.1960. Pastel. 14in x 10½in.*

medium throughout the period 1955-1970. For her they had the immense advantage of permitting her to leave work and pick it up again without having to wash brushes, remix paint and make allowances for colour changes due to drying. It was not, however, pressure of time alone which persuaded Peggy to make the change. Although pastels are notoriously difficult to handle, in the right hands they

Aldeburgh beach, red lady.
Early 1960s. Pastel.
10in x 17in.

Orange chair, fruit and flowers. *Pastel. 14in x 10½in. Peggy had two such wooden chairs which she painted herself.*

Summer, Aldeburgh. *c.1960. Oil on canvas. 18½in x 31in. Castle Museum, Norwich.*

can produce, like no other medium, the most miraculous effects – the bloom of a fresh peach, the down on the skin of a child, the coloured dust on the velvet of a butterfly wing. For flowers they are incomparable, as Peggy was to find; for anything delicate, soft, subtle, fresh, misty, ethereal, tender, youthful, they can work like a dream; but turn to sombre, sublime, profound, elevated, aggressive, tormented, dramatic, even passionate, and they generally look absurdly out of place.

This suited Peggy for she had no wish to be profound, at least not in her painting. But make no mistake, the emotional input, the imagination, sensibility, artistic intelligence, skill and forethought needed to create what is transparently beautiful is no less than is required for a statement that is disturbing. Indeed, it is usually the superficial mind that seeks to impress by rhetoric. There is no greater absurdity than the present day notion that art must challenge. Challenge for what? To build or destroy? Great art illuminates through subtle persuasion and not by crude confrontation Peggy, and Harry also, subscribed to the Matisse doctrine: 'There is no necessity for the spectator to analyse, that would be to arrest his attention and not to release it. Ideally he should allow himself, without knowing it, to be engaged by the mechanism of the picture. Expression for me is not to be found in the passion which blazes from a face or is evident in some violent gesture. It is in the whole disposition of the picture.'

It was, however, the work of Bonnard rather than Matisse which appealed most to Peggy and which led Harry to comment in February 1960, 'I think you are somehow related to Bonnard.' The Bonnard exhibition at the Royal Academy in 1966 confirmed this commitment. Peggy called it, '. . . a glimpse of Heaven.' The task Matisse and Bonnard had both set themselves, and where Peggy was a

Suffolk coast near Sizewell. *Early 1960s. Pastel.*
10in x17½ in.

follower, was to achieve maximum density of colour without retreating into purely flat, two-dimensional, design. It was a tight rope, an exceedingly difficult balancing act, but they succeeded through subtleties of handling and inspired colour juxtaposition. Peggy also believed there was much to be learnt from Braque, and among those closer to her in age she was a great admirer of Anne Redpath (1895-1965)', whom she knew slightly.

Peggy's approach to painting was more physical, more down-to-earth, than has sometimes been suggested. She sought, not 'the essence which hides behind the shape' as one writer has claimed, but the essence of the shape itself. Towards the end of her all-too-short life, to help make ends meet, she occasionally took on pupils on a one-to-one basis and she would point to her stomach and tell them that this is where it lies, not up in the heavens. We would be wrong to see her as a mystic, a seeker after symbols and invisible meanings. She was a lover of what is here and now, and did not ask for more. As she wrote in an appeal for help from the Artists' General Benevolent Institute, 'the visual world, be it in pure landscape, skies, figures, flowers, fruit, all objects held in space and light, is for me an ever growing source of delight and wonder.' Art for her was a celebration and a thanksgiving. In 1950 she had written to her mother, 'I wish you would write something Mother, a tiny book of your childhood. No - don't say you can't - that is nonsense, write from the heart, just as simple as that, just as you have always told me. I think it would give you a great sense of satisfaction, because all creative work is a prayer of thanksgiving to God.'

Peggy was always an avid reader and, throughout her life, her sketchbooks were covered in verse and passages of prose, some her own but mostly from the poets she loved, Donne, Hopkins, Clare, Traherne, Shelley, Keats, Brontë, Christina Rosetti, Rilke and many others. It seemed as if she found writing helped her to maintain the creative momentum and it gave her a sense of solidarity, that she was among friends. Never once, however, did these writings have any recognisable connection with what she was painting or drawing. The notion of translating or

Green parasol. *c.1960.*
Pastel. 9¾in x 10¼in. Castle Museum, Norwich.

Suffolk lane in the snow.
A classic oil painting of the mid 1960s. Oil on board. 13in x 16in.

Sunshades on the beach at Aldeburgh.
Mid 1960s.
Oil on canvas.
15½in x 22in.

Young horsewomen.
c.1960. Pastel.
12in x 18in.

***Aldeburgh beach**. Mid 1960s. Sepia drawing. 7½in x 13in.*

***Landscape in Provence.** Mid 1960s. Pastel. 5½in x 8½in.*

***Provençal bulls.** Mid 1960s. Sepia drawing. 11½in x 15in.*

Beauchene, Harry Morton Colvile's villa in Provence where Peggy stayed in the summer of 1964 and 1966.

Geraldine at Beauchene.

interpreting from one art form to another was anathema. If what she was doing could not stand on its own feet, it did not deserve to exist. Every experience had to be fully absorbed and then recreated on its own terms. She was also a great lover of music and the same rationale applied – it simply enriched her creative life. Allied to her distaste for interpretation was her life-long rejection of imitation. On one of her sketches she quoted Tchekov: 'I can only write from memory and I have never written directly from nature. The subject must first seep through in memory, as in a filter, leaving only what is important and typical.' Substitute 'paint' for 'write' and this could well have been Peggy's epitaph.

As Peggy had no car, and had never learnt to drive, and as she and her mother were more than ever isolated in the depth of the country, the 1960s saw her increasingly dependent on selling her pictures locally. This she did through small galleries in Ipswich, Hintlesham, Felixstowe, Woodbridge, Saxmundham, Yoxford, Aldeburgh, Walberswick, Lavenham and Sudbury and also, more importantly, by direct sales to a few private customers. On one occasion, August 1964, she held a joint exhibition with Harry in Aldeburgh but it was only a modest success. After the opening she did not in fact remain with it because Harry and Geraldine had invited

Vineyard, Provence.
Late 1960s. Pastel.
8in x 11½in.

Houses in Provence.
Showing the influence of Cézanne. Late 1960s.
Watercolour. 11in x 15in.

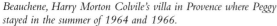

River landscape.
Oil on canvas. 10½in x 13½in.
Seemingly a view in France in the late 1960s.

Beauchene. *Pastel.*
14in x 10½in.

Moon through buildings.
Provence. Late 1960s.
Pastel. 8½in x 7½in.

Fredrickswood in winter. *In the woods near Dunwich, the Suffolk home of Alan and Elizabeth Ivimey.*
Late 1960s. Oil on board. 22in x 28in.

Fruit on a plate.
Pastel. 10½in x 14½in. The resonance of colour Peggy could obtain from the pastel medium is indeed remarkable. A work of the 1960s.

Alan Ivimey *– ink drawing. Late 1960s. 6in x 4½in.*

Alan Ivimey, earlier days. Photograph taken to promote the publication of his book Any Fine Saturday.

her to stay with them at Beauchene, their house in Provence. This was her first visit to France since 1947. She was on the most cordial terms with Geraldine as indeed she was with the wives of all her special male friends. Peggy made a second visit in 1966, and then not again until 1971. Her movements were restricted on account of looking after mother, although Rosemary, who was working in a school in Northumberland, was able to release her during the school holidays. The devotion and support of her elder sister meant much to Peggy and would subsequently be a crucial factor in bringing her work to the notice of a wider public.

It was at another exhibition in Aldeburgh on 30th July 1965, a mixed exhibition, arranged by the Aldeburgh Festival in which she was taking part, that Peggy came to know Alan and Elizabeth Ivimey. She discovered that they lived in the woods behind Dunwich, only some four miles away, and soon they were seeing a great deal of each other. They would pick Peggy up, sometimes as many as two or three times a week, go shopping, visit the cinema (usually at Aldeburgh), have meals together, attend concerts, walk on the beach and tour the countryside. As often as not, the day would end with Alan taking Peggy back to the Stone House and by the end of September she was writing in her diary, '. . . one of the happiest days of my life – back through the lanes – thank God.'

It was, Rosemary noticed, a rather different relationship from the other three, there was no longer the slightest sense of the awe-struck countrygirl, it was essentially a partnership between equals. Alan was highly sophisticated, with a tremendous sense of humour. He was a journalist, the first compère of *Woman's Hour*, with a number of books to his credit, on the history of London, Pepys, Madame Curie, and *Who slept here?* (about English Country Houses). While ultimately nobody could really replace Harry, and Peggy's admiration for Alik was unsurpassed, she felt a certain ease with Alan. Her ambitions were now lower as no longer had she set her sights on marrying and having children. To have a friend, a good and highly entertaining friend just round the corner, was all she could hope

Flowers in a window at night. *Pencil and watercolour. 1969. 14in x 10in. Castle Museum, Norwich.*

Alan Ivimey. Late 1960s.

Peggy. c.1970.

for. Her diary entries show, above all, a sense of relief that she was no longer isolated and rejected. It was a friendship which lasted until Alan died in August 1973.

It is difficult to say how far it was mere chance and how much a radical preference which led Peggy towards older men who, as it happens, were already happily married. Certainly, she had received offers from those who were closer to her in age and were unattached. Her looks were attractive, her disposition warm and lively. Like her mother, who had perhaps been prettier, she took much care about her personal presentation. Her passport reveals she was five feet two inches tall, had brown eyes and light brown hair. She could speak with wit and enthusiasm on many subjects and, despite her natural reserve, she was never reticent in her approach to men in whom she was interested. Her overall attitude may have had something to do with her having four elder brothers, at least two of whom were quite dominant personalities. Her upbringing was such as to instil respect, if not subservience, towards the male sex. Or was it, quite simply, that she was bored by men of her own age?

Girl in blue. *Pastel. 8½in x 7½in. A sketch of the early 1970s.*

CHAPTER IV
Last Years

In the autumn of 1966 Peggy first suspected that she had cancer. Although she was to die from this nine years later, there were many ups and downs on the way and, in spite of the examinations, operations and treatment, she often felt quite well and was optimistic. She was wonderfully sustained by her faith and her painting, which had never been richer in quality and quantity, reaching a peak around 1969-72. She now seemed to know what she wanted and how to achieve it. A particular inspiration was the possession of her own studio. With a loan from

Sweetpeas. *1970. Pastel. 16½in x 14½in. One of the pictures with which Peggy celebrated her new studio.*

Peggy's studio at the Stone House after conversion and the interior, 1970.

John Curzon (of Lockington Hall) and the help of Eric Sandon, a close architect friend of many years standing, a derelict outbuilding in the Stone House garden was converted into a relatively large and wholly agreeable place for her to produce, in her last years, some of her finest and most personal work. Although not completed until January 1970, even its promise seemed to inspire her.

Another factor was the death of her mother in February 1971 at the age of ninety-two. Never for one moment had Peggy begrudged the years caring for her.

As a child she had written a poem which began:

Of all the things I have in the world
My mother is best of all...

And when she was fifteen she wrote:

To Mother.

Once there lived a mother squirrel
With softest hair a silvery grey
She had several sons and daughters
All but two lived far away

She was good this mother squirrel
Cared for them with patience sweet
Times were hard and she kept wondering
What she should give them to eat

Soon the Autumn winds will wander
Through the mellow sunlit woods
There'll be nuts to seek and gather
Sticks for burning, fruit for food

We will gather round the camp fire
Watch the blue smoke curl and fly
Watch it lingering in the tree tops
Then pass on towards the sky

Whether rich or poor
Happiness we'll always find
Beauty is our friend for ever
To bring contentment to the mind

Here I send a little present
Gathered in the wood maybe
Store it Squirrey in your store room
Keep it safe for you and me

You have friends dear all around you
Friends who love you and adore
All your goodness, all your sweetness
That is all - I can't say more

Their relationship had always been exceptionally loving.

In a letter some twenty years later she would write, 'I shall never forget all the

Sunflowers. *1971. Watercolour. 23½in x 16in. Peggy painted several large scale watercolours during her last years.*

Autumn Daisies. *Early 1970s. Pastel. 16in x 10in.*

difficult things we have lived through together . . . your love and care when we were unwell . . . the firelight in the room and your gentle touch and footstep. It was enough just to have you there, and you never denied us your love and care whenever we wanted it. I can never thank you enough or tell you what it means to me . . . and the wonderful thing is I feel the same still. Your spirit will always be a bright star for me, your companionship beyond expression.'

Peggy was, of course, the apple of her parents' eye and everyone knew it. Yet, thanks to their discipline and the privations, she was never pampered and happily she and Rosemary, potentially the most threatened, were soon close friends. What it did was to give her a profound sense of security which, in later years, helped to carry her through many crises. From her father she had acquired an ethic of conscientious craft and work. Again and again she would say and write, 'All I can do is very simply to work,' or, for instance, 'the best of the day has gone but I must work all the same.' Although it was holidays for others, for her it would always be – 'but they know I must work.' She had learnt only too well that what is called 'inspiration' does not come uninvited, that it presents itself only to those who have prepared the way, who have fed the mind with whatever is relevant and who are alert enough to recognise its credentials when eventually it does appear. The driving force was not ambition for herself but the determination to justify the faith her father and mother and later others, had placed in her. She could not

Still life with books. *Oil on canvas. 18½in x 22½in. An opulent work looking back to her style of the mid 1950s.*

Rockforms. *Pastel 3¼in x 7¼in. A small sketch which reveals the quintessence of her style of the 1970s.*

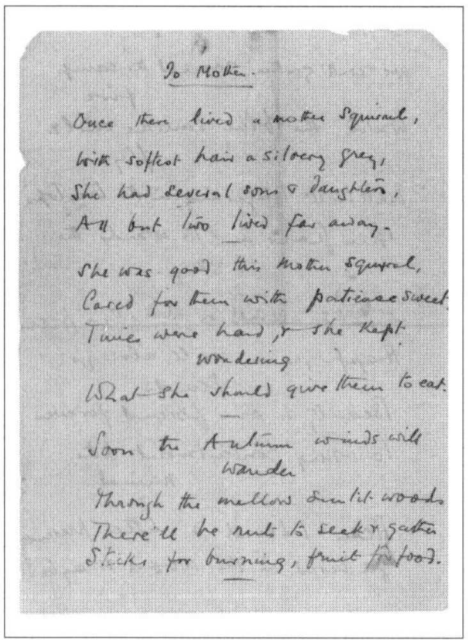

To Mother.

Once there lived a mother Squirrel,
With softest hair a silvery grey,
She had several sons & daughters,
All but two lived far away.

She was good this Mother Squirrel,
Cared for them with patience sweet,
Times were hard, & she kept wondering
What she should give them to eat.

Soon the Autumn winds will wander
Through the mellow sunlit woods
There'll be nuts to seek & gather
Sticks for burning, fruit for food.

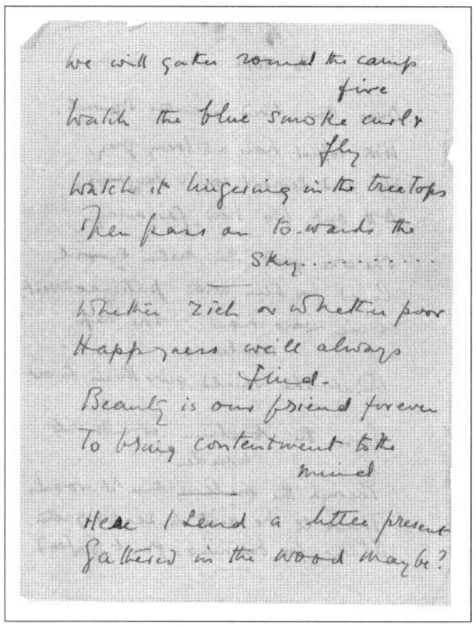

We will gather round the camp fire
Watch the blue smoke curl & fly
Watch it lingering in the treetops
Then pass on towards the sky.........

Whether rich or whether poor
Happiness we'll always find.
Beauty is our friend forever
To bring contentment to the mind

Here I send a little present
Gathered in the wood maybe?

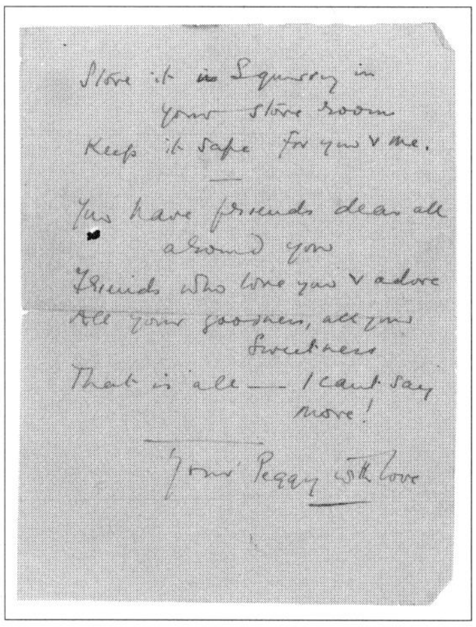

Store it Squirrey in your store room
Keep it safe for you & me.

You have friends dear all around you
Friends who love you & adore
All your goodness, all your sweetness
That is all — I can't say more!

Your Peggy with love

Peggy's poem to her mother, written when she was fifteen.

***Rolling Fields**. c.1971. Oil on board. 18in x 24in.*

disappoint them or waste the talent she knew she had. Again to her mother, 'Before I die I would like to put down something worthy of this love for beauty you have given me and which we so joyously share.'

Nonetheless her mother's death gave Peggy greater freedom to concentrate on working in her much-loved new studio. She suspected her time was limited but this was a spur as well as an anxiety. To make ends meet she found it preferable to

***Norfolk Farmlands.** 1971. Oil on panel. 14in x 22in.*

The Fens of Lincolnshire. *As seen from the train on her journey to Northumberland in 1972. Watercolour. 4¾in x 6¾in.*

Moon over the garden. *Pastel. 8in x 10in. A late work showing the influence of Bonnard (see pages 64 and 65).*

From simple things, a show of sheer magic

PAINTING often runs in families and the name of Somerville is a well-established one in the art world. Peggy Somerville studied under her father Charles Somerville, together with her brother Stuart, whose flower paintings are a feature of many exhibitions.

At the age of 12 her work attracted the attention of Walter Sickert and she went on to study at the Royal Academy schools. Solo exhibitions at Claridges and the Beaux Arts Gallery and group shows at other London galleries established her reputation as an artist.

The unique quality of her paintings and drawings is such that it is best appreciated in a one-man show, so the exhibition she is now showing at the gallery owned by another brother—Forbes Somerville — in Saxmundham is not to be missed.

The effect of sheer magic that Peggy Somerville manages to conjure from simple things is such that one feels the world must be a good place if such gentle wonders are around us.

Grapes in a bowl, flowers with a presence all their own and those fleeting moments that leave an image on the memory for ever, such as figures in front of a window, horses and riders against green or the explosive power of Provencal bulls, come from their frames and impress with the same intensity of feeling that the artist must have felt when she painted them.

Peggy Somerville uses oil, water colours and pastels but her colour sense is completely at home and able to make the most out of whatever medium she is using. Never thin or repetitive, her colour is completely her own and whether she is working in the creamy opaques of the oils or the singing darks and brilliance of the pastels there is an original approach that is as justified a part of the picture-making as it is charming to look at.

How often it is forgotten that pictures do provide pleasure and delight to the spectator, and there is certainly much to be found in this exhibition which is pure delight. Which does not mean that there is any playing down of serious values. Artistic integrity is to be found in every work.

One is not asked to just enjoy the beauty of her art as a graphic and immediate sensation and then pass on. It is necessary to linger at each picture to allow it to develop. The eye first takes in glowing patches of colour, perhaps on a neck or end of a house but before it registers as a patch of colour the picture becomes crystal clear. Creating order from apparent confusion, slowly one can respond to the relationships in the picture and contours emerge.

Peggy Somerville at the Somerville Gallery, Saxmundham, where she has an exhibition of her paintings and drawings until June 24.

The coloured patches also weave a web of air and space so that, as with a good drawing, the pictures can be read slowly in time and what appears cursory strokes of brush or pastel develop into a well-defined form.

This characteristic is most marked in some of the figure drawings in pastel which break more definitely with traditional composition. The landscape work takes a more orthodox route along a receding perspective but in these pastels she implies space by more adventurous means and manages to suggest the unexpected, sometimes aerial, viewpoint so that the viewer can feel like a moth circling within the picture.

The exhibition closes on June 24.

Peggy 1973.

The newspaper review of her 1972 Saxmundham exhibition.

Head of a girl. *c.1973. Blue biro and pastel on envelope. 6½in x 4½in. Shows how Peggy made use of any medium and support which happened to be on hand. Castle Museum, Norwich.*

take on a few pupils on a one-to-one basis, rather than spend her time hawking her pictures round the galleries. Now that she had her studio the teaching was more practicable. She charged two guineas for an hour and three for two hours; for a course of twelve lessons the price was twenty guineas. Meanwhile her brother Forbes had switched from farming to art dealing and, in 1972 and 1974, he arranged two successful solo exhibitions in his gallery in Saxmundham. Forty

Still life, fruit and flowers. *Oil on board. 14in x 17½in. Characteristic of her oil painting style of the 1970s.*

out of seventy-one pictures were sold at the first exhibition and another twenty-two from sixty-four at the second, when prices were higher. She was not showing her most recent work but that going back as much as twenty years or more. As so often happens it had taken the public time to catch up with her. She was, of course, delighted.

In many ways the work of her last phase can be seen as a reprise, a summing up of all that had gone before. While pastels still remained her primary medium, she returned strongly to both oils and watercolour. She pursued further than ever before the disengagement of form and colour, the distillation of all the disparate ingredients of her art. Her handling, always free and expressive, came to assume an added quality, with every movement like that of a great dancer. We are reminded of Berthe Morisot, while Bloomsbury looks clumsy by comparison. It could be said she was moving towards abstraction, but this would only be a half-truth. She understood only too well the importance of what are nowadays called abstract values, but for her they were only the means towards the end. The job of the artist was to solve a problem, the problem of how to present actuality without

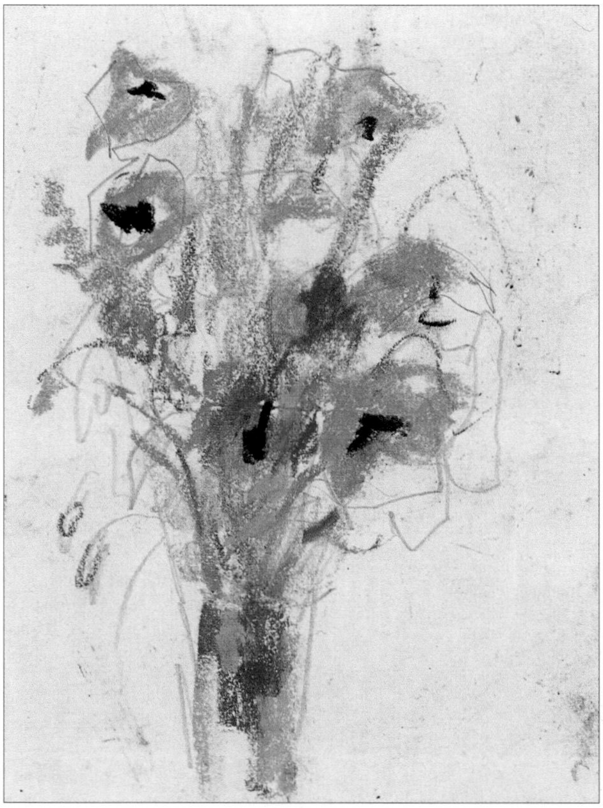

Poppies. *c.1973. Pastel. 5in x 4in.*

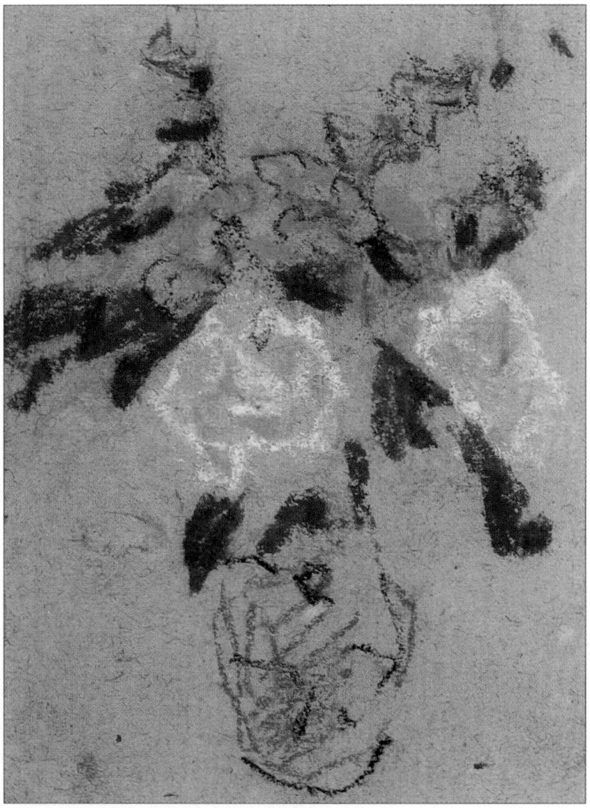

Roses *c.1973. Pastel.*

Vases of flowers. *1973.*
Pastel. 9in x 13in.

Mother and child. *Sepia wash. 10in x 8in.*

sacrificing formal values. To pursue one at the expense of the other was a negation of the essential artistic process. Besides Peggy was too much a lover of nature to be able to deny it; it would have been a betrayal of her innermost feelings. Nonetheless exercises in abstraction could be useful, and her occasional Braque-like paintings may be seen in this sense.

To describe Peggy's art as feminine is a compliment not a stricture. There is a French art, a British art, a Dutch art, a Spanish art. Why not a masculine art and a feminine art? It is true there has never been a feminine tradition and that allegiance to time and place has been far stronger than attachment to gender; and it is true also that virtually every aspect of artistic expression is equally accessible to performers of either sex. To misquote Shakespeare: 'Hath they not eyes, hands, organs, dimensions, senses, affections, passions? Fed with the same food, hurt with

The church at Middleton. *Pastel. 7in x 10in.*

the same weapons, subject to the same diseases, healed by the same means, warmed and cooled by the same winter and summer? If you prick them, do they not bleed? If you tickle them, do they not laugh?' And yet of course there is a difference, and it would be sheer perversity to attempt to divorce what is enchanting, tender, graceful, everything that Peggy so wonderfully dispensed, from the person she was. She could turn to other styles, as indeed she did for a time in the 1930s, but she preferred to be herself and for this we can only be grateful.

Peggy had by now learnt to take all things with equanimity. Geraldine, Harry's wife, had died suddenly in June 1969, and it is just possible it may have entered Peggy's head that she and Harry might get together for old times' sake. It therefore came as something of a shock when Harry announced in April 1971 that he was going to marry a distant cousin of Geraldine's. It did not in fact materialise, and the put-down made only a momentary impression. Later in the same year she made her third and last visit to Beauchene, this time accompanied by Stuart's eldest son John and one of her pupils, Barbara Willis. It seems they had a riotous time, though more so on the journey than while staying in the grand old but dilapidated villa. Meanwhile, Peggy's own health was deteriorating and she was much saddened by Alan's death in 1973. The wives of two of her other former flames died during the early 1970s, Rodolfa Kouveld and Zoia Poklewski. Peggy had throughout kept in close touch with them and it was indeed the source of much happiness that this warmth of friendship was sustained.

Picnic. *c.1973. Watercolour. 9½in x 15½in. Peggy's eldest sister Nancy.*

Peggy was on the last lap, and she knew it. Yet her eyes remained open to new possibilities and she was always positive. After her successful Saxmundham exhibition in 1972, she visited Rosemary in Northumberland and together they went to see a 'quite wonderful' Anne Redpath exhibition in Edinburgh. At once she would paint a pastiche. This was not imitation not plagiarism, but a tribute, a recognition that another artist had opened a door, a mine shaft, in the hope that others would use it. It is a characteristic of Peggy's sensibility that she was deeply sympathetic and understanding of other modes of expression, especially those

Old Houses. *Anne Redpath, Corsica 1959.*

Farm buildings, Northumberland. *1972. Watercolour. 10in x11½in. Shows the influence of Anne Redpath whose paintings she had just seen at an exhibition in Edinburgh.*

Child with flowers. *Early 1970s. Pastel. 20in x 14½in.*

Harry in 1972.

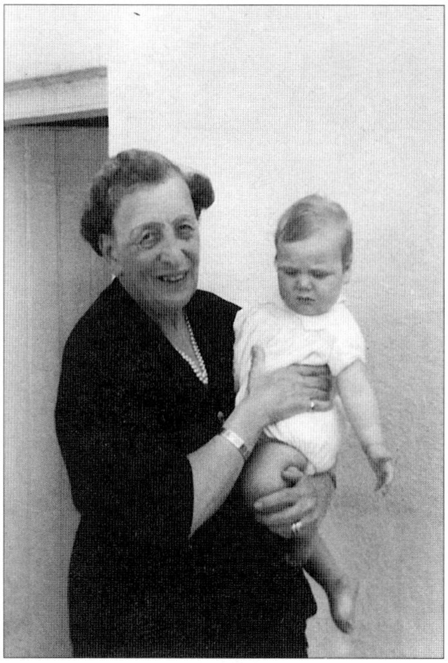

Zoia Poklewski with grandson in 1966.

Rodolfa Kouveld and Charles Kouveld at Kingston in 1953.

with which she felt an affinity. One of the most striking symptoms of this was the way in which her handwriting changed according to the dominant influence at any given time; it was like Stuart's in the mid-1930s, Kouveld's in the late 1930s and early 1940s and like Harry's in the late 1940s and beyond. Her journey to Northumberland also reminds us of the speed with which she responded to what she saw. As she had remarked to her mother many years before, 'I always think the country seen from a fast moving train is especially inviting. One knows one must gaze on it only for a moment and then it is gone.' She would make quick pencil

Llanthony Priory in Wales which Peggy visited with her brother Forbes and his wife Nesta in September, 1973.

Peggy at her 1974 exhibition in Saxmundham. The child on her lap is Camilla, daughter of Mary, one of her nieces. Above Peggy, on the right, is a painting of her mother from the 1950s.

On the waterfront. *Sepia wash. 8in x 11in.*

sketches from the window and paint them afterwards from memory, in this case, 'Across the fens of Lincolnshire . . . like satin ribbons the cabbage fields stretching away, purple and blue – dark purple earth, stubble where flocks of birds feed,' and onwards, 'the landscape flying by and the ceaseless rhythm of the train . . . This is Yorkshire where my father spent part of his youth and found my mother, fresh as a flower . . . There is a kind of poetry in desolation, where man has been and gone and left his scar in the grey cities of the North.' Peggy was a true Impressionist!

In September 1973, following a spell in hospital, Peggy accepted an invitation from Forbes and his wife Nesta to join them on a fortnight's visit to Wales: 'I am feeling like a child about to make a journey west – to see new things and I hope to revisit a place I love, Llanthony.' She had known it from a fleeting, semi-clandestine, excursion with Kouveld in the 1940s. 'To return to that place moved me deeply . . . Long ago I walked through these hills and bathed in the mountain streams . . . What centuries have heard these rivers sing, since first the Christians built this monument to God . . . Ruined buildings under high trees – Claude Lorrain everywhere, wonderful contours, twists and turns of lane, ancient trees, some flourishing still, some dying, still beautiful, ponies resting beside a grey stone wall, light on distant hills, patches of red earth, bracken, blue shadows, water rich amber . . . rooks and jackdaws calling in high places.' No, she was not complaining. She had had a full and happy life and she could only be grateful for it.

A splash of flowers. *Watercolour.* $7\frac{1}{4}$*in x* $10\frac{3}{4}$*in. In the totally liberated style of the 1970s.*

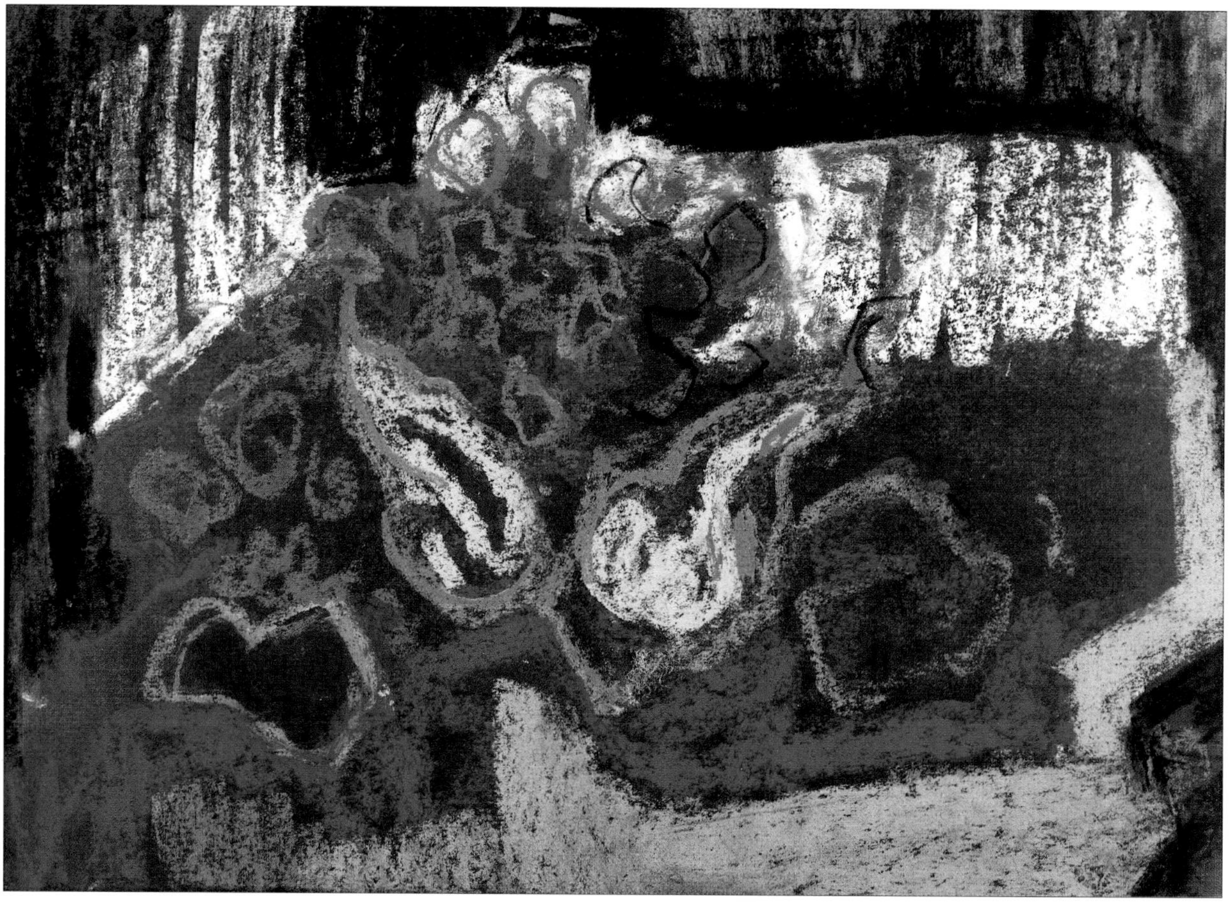

Pears and Grapes. *Pastel.* $10\frac{1}{2}$ *x 14in. Peggy had seen and been much affected by the Braque exhibition at the Edinburgh Festival in 1956, but it was not until 1972/3 that she made a few sorties down that particular road. Renewed interest in the work of Anne Redpath may also have been a factor here.*

Irises in white jug. *Watercolour. 15in x 11in. In the explosive style of the final years 1972-1974.*

Towards the end of 1974 she was too ill to continue painting and Rosemary came to be with her. The end was close and in June 1975 she heard from Harry:

My darling Peggy,

A letter from John brings your message. It moves me deeply and I am at a loss how to tell you all the thoughts in my old heart. Useless to say how distressed I am at what, I know, is an understatement. Dearest Peggy, I want you to know I am with you and that I would give anything to take your pains upon myself so that a much better artist and an infinitely greater being should be relieved and free to work in peace. You are always with me in my studio. Two pictures you know well, one I painted on that bench in the orchard I had built for the purpose, another little one where you are seated on the grass; both are faceless, but it seems to me they both express something of your loveliness. A third picture you have never seen, since it was painted after your last visit with John and Barbara; it always faces me when I am at my easel and is a real portrait painted on one of those mahogany panels Stuart used to have; it is very much alive and always gives me the feeling that you are watching my efforts with kind interest.

Almost forty years since we met in the Glebe Place Studio, when a deep affection started and survived so many years and events. And today is your birthday my dearest Peggy. I cannot imagine new wishes, more of them, than those I always make for you.

I know also how unworthy I have been of the wonderful affection you have always given me, and I know too that you have forgiven any wrong. Darling, I have not done it for many years, but I will try and pray that your pains should stop.

God bless you, my love and kisses.

H.

On the morning of Sunday June the 29th she died.

Remembering a painter whose death made 1975 a sad year

Peggy Somerville with some of her paintings in her Saxmundham studio. The picture was taken in 1972.

Before we start on the New Year I feel sure I should not miss the opportunity to look back at 1975. And to look back at one of the saddest events of the year — the death of Peggy Somerville.

Although she was ever-retiring in character and called herself "primarily a recluse" her place in the art world of East Anglia will not easily be filled.

The last five years of her life were hampered by the illness which became final but her painting was her strength. Until I recently visited her studio, which still stands as she left it, I had not realised the extent of her lifetime devotion to art.

I saw water colours and drawings made when she was three years old, at the time when she first exhibited at the Royal Drawing Society. The maturity and sophistication of these is beyond what one imagines even child prodigies maybe expected to produce.

She felt she owed a great debt to her painter father and her mother, a poet. Even given the sympathetic background and opportunity to paint at this early age this still does not explain her prodigious talent for composing, for drawing in a sketchy landscape full of movement and vivacity at a time when most children are satisfied with producing a matchstick man.

At seven, Peggy Somerville was exhibiting at the Royal Irish Academy, and at the ripe age of nine she held her first one-man show at The Claridge Gallery in London which was rapidly followed by a number of other exhibitions where her work attracted the attention of Sickert and Matthew Smith. For the study of life drawing she attended the Royal Academy schools in 1939 but then the war came and she served five years in the Women's Land Army. Later she spent 11 years caring for her elderly mother so that her painting career was far from plain sailing.

Although born in Middlesex, Peggy Somerville moved to Suffolk while still a young child and it was this county and France which most influenced her painting. Her Scottish ancestry of course provided links with France and these were very strong in her artistic life.

Many visits to Provence must have heightened her appreciation of warm but bright and glowing colour. This colour (which is never lurid) is what came to symbolise Peggy's painting for me. This was her beautiful intimate choice of subject.

Flowers are common enough currency in the painting world, and she frequently painted them in oil and water colour and drew them in pastel. But they were flowers taken on their own terms.

She never made them coy and decorative nor did she torture them into formal settings. They were shown through her sensitive appreciation of their individual characters and a sense of the wonder of nature. That may sound trite but there is nothing trite in her work, what can be felt is a profound respect for flowers, the landscape or whatever human situation she painted.

She was content to interpret this on to her paper or canvas without moralising or delivering a strident message.

As I looked through her pictures I had the same feeling as when I had visited her exhibitions. A reassuring optimism, a tranquility throughout the pictures — I doubt if she ever painted a troubled work in her life – and a feeling that she could not have been other than this.

She was being true to herself and her vision of life in her interior scenes, or the casual little views of the countryside and beach are one artist's song.

Her optimism, and, I feel, an innocent faith in the best things of life, made her an outstanding artist even without her truly exceptional talent. Her gentle serenity made her someone who was able to communicate successfully through her person or her art. She will be greatly missed.

Freda Constable

A final tribute by the art correspondent of the East Anglian Daily Times.

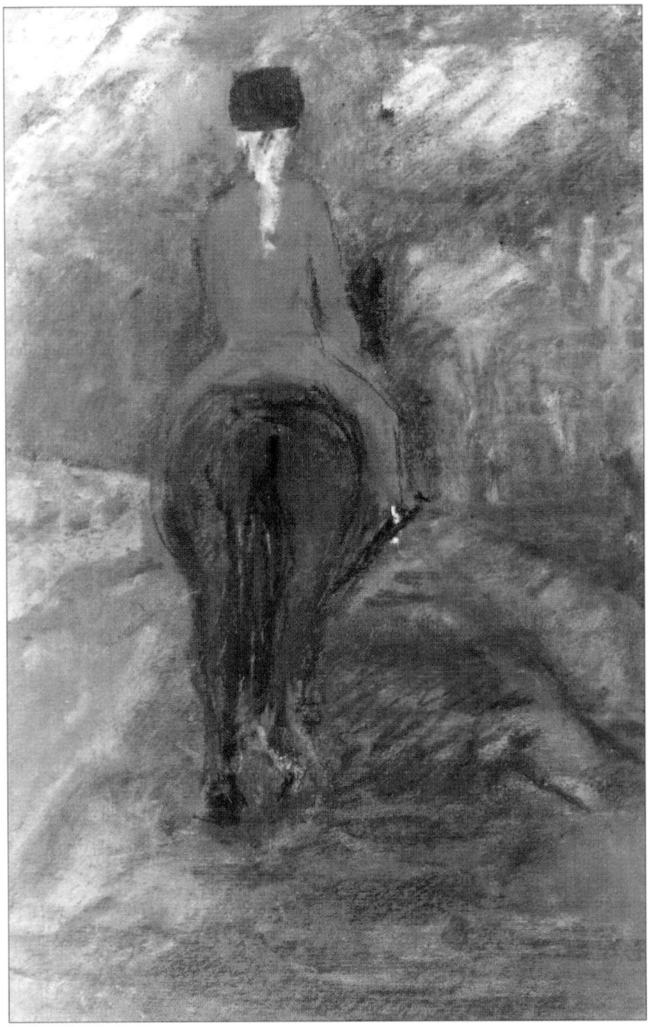

Child on horseback.
Pastel.

Chronology

1918	2 June. Born, the Old Ford Farm, Ashford, Middlesex.
1922	1 April. Two watercolours at the annual exhibition of the Royal Drawing Society, the Guildhall, London.
1924	First oil paintings.
1927	February. 'Happy days by the sea' at the New Irish Salon, Dublin.
1928	February. Two watercolours at the New Irish Salon. 7–23 June. Retrospective at the Claridge Gallery, opened by Sir John Lavery.
1929	17 July–2 August. Second exhibition at the Claridge Gallery opened by Lady Lavery. Four pictures bought by Mrs Sloane, an American, later given to the Hermitage Foundation, Norfolk, Virginia. September. 'The cornfield' hung at the R.O.I.
1931	Parents moved to Shimpling, mid Suffolk.
1932	21 November–3 December. Solo exhibition at the Beaux Arts Gallery, London. A painting bought by Walter Sickert.
1934	Parents moved to Cavendish, mid Suffolk.
1936	June–December. Six months stay in Holland. Parents moved to Wiggington near Tring, where rejoined by Peggy.
1937	October. Two Dutch paintings at the R.O.I.
1939	29 May. Peggy's father died. Studied as a probationer at the Royal Academy Schools for six weeks only. War declared. Peggy took a job on the land.
1942	Formally recruited into the Women's Land Army.
1944	October–November. Exhibited at the R.O.I. December–January 1945. Exhibited at the R.B.A.
1945	7 September. Released from the Land Army. Moved with her mother from Wiggington to her brother Stuart's house at Newbourne near Woodbridge, Suffolk. Renewed friendship with Harry Morton Colvile.

1947	August–October. Two months in France, mostly at Château Bannay near Bourges.
1951	11–28 September. Solo exhibition at the Beaux Arts Gallery 1953.
1953	August. First of three visits to the Pembroke coast with the family of her brother Forbes. The others were in 1955 and 1956. Peggy also went to Cornwall with them in 1954.
1955	Exhibited with Harry Morton Colvile and six other artists at Wildenstein. First of several visits to Aldeburgh, staying with Juliet Laden.
1956	Began work on model railway landscape background at Lockington Hall, Derbyshire. (Work continued at intervals until 1959.) September. To Rannoch Moor, Scotland, as part of the project.
1957	Met Alik and Zoia Powklewski at Lockington Hall.
1960	Moved with her mother to rented property (Hill House) at Westleton near Dunwich.
1962	November. Alik Powklewski died.
1963	April. Death of Charles Kouveld, her close friend since 1932.
1964	Joint exhibition with Harry at Festival Gallery, Aldeburgh. July. moved with her mother to The Stone House, Middleton. August. Stayed with the Colviles at Beauchêne in Provence.
1965	July. Came to know Alan and Elizabeth Ivimey.
1966	August. Second visit to Beauchêne.
1968	Appealed for and received help from the Artists' General Benevolent Institute (AGBI).
1969	September. To Amsterdam to see Rembrandt exhibition. December. Conversion of outhouse into studio completed.
1970	November. Hospital treatment for cancer.
1971	February. Peggy's mother died aged 92. September. Third visit to Beauchêne.
1972	5–24 June. Successful exhibition at her brother Forbes's Somerville Gallery at Saxmundham, Suffolk. September. Stayed with Rosemary in Northumberland.
1973	June. Major cancer operation. September. Visited Wales with Forbes and his wife Nesta.
1974	March. Again to Northumberland.

10–29 June. Second exhibition Somerville Gallery, Saxmundham.

1975 29 June. Peggy died of cancer.

1977 10–26 June. Memorial exhibition at the Aldeburgh Festival.
Eight pictures from Peggy's estate given to the Castle Museum, Norwich.

1985 Forty-eight further pictures bequeathed to the Castle Museum, Norwich.
20 July–26 January 1986. Exhibition at the Museum to celebrate this bequest.

1986 February. Exhibition transferred to Gainsborough's House, Sudbury.

1989 Anglia Television programme devoted to the artist.

1990 Exhibition at the International Monetary Fund, Washington.
Publication of *The Child Art of Peggy Somerville.*

1991 June. Exhibition at the David Messum Gallery. Others have followed.

1994 June. Second Aldeburgh Festival Exhibition.

The tramp.
Oil on board. Aged twelve.

Peggy at the table. c.1950

Bibliography

As most of the literature about Peggy Somerville has so far been linked to her exhibitions, this list has been arranged chronologically. Many of the early reviews are in fact no more than duplicated news items; detailed dates have not, therefore, been given. A full dossier is held by the Castle Museum, Norwich.

1928 June. Claridge Gallery I. Foreword by Hugh Stokes.
Reviews: *Morning Post*; a second notice appeared on 18 June; *The Times*; *Daily Mirror*; *Daily Sketch*; *Daily News*; *The People*; *News of the World*; *Christian Herald*; *Evening Standard*; *Evening News*; *The Star*; *Illustrated London News*; *World Art Weekly*; *Woman's Pictorial*; *Apollo* (August); *Titbits*; *Birmingham Post*; *Birmingham Mail*; *Bristol Evening News*; *Eastern Daily Press* (two notices); *Glasgow Bulletin*; *Glasgow Herald*; *Liverpool Post*; *Manchester Dispatch*; *Newcastle Evening Chronicle*; *Weekly Scotsman*.

Christian Science Monitor, Boston; *Western Mail* (Australia); *Ceylon Morning Leader*; *Times of India*; *Melbourne Age*; *Cape Times*; *Allahabad Pioneer*; *Saskatoon Star*; *Wellington Journal* (N.Z.).

1929 July. Claridge Gallery II. Foreword by Hugh Stokes.
Reviews: *The Times*; *Morning Post*; *Evening Standard*; *Bath Chronicle*; *Birmingham Gazette*; *Birmingham Mail*; *Bolton Evening News*; *Bristol Evening Times*; *Burton Evening Gazette*; *Cheshire Daily Echo*; *Craven Herald*; *East Anglian Daily Times*; *Eastern Daily Press*; *Eastern Evening News*; *Dundee Advertiser*; *Glasgow Bulletin*; *Glasgow Evening News*; *Grimsby Telegraph*; *Halifax Daily Courier*; *Ipswich Evening Star*; *Leicester Mercury*; *Lincoln Echo*; *Midland Daily Telegraph*; *Notts Journal*; *Oldham Evening Chronicle*; *Scarborough Evening News*; *Sheffield Independent*; *Somerset Guardian*; *South Wales Evening Express*; *Swindon Evening Advertiser*; *Sunderland Echo*; *Wiltshire News*; *Yorkshire Evening Press*.

Cape Argus (SA); *Cork Examiner*; *Adelaide Register*; *Natal Advertiser*; *Winnipeg Evening Tribune*; *Shanghai Times*.

1932 November. Beaux Arts Gallery I. Foreword by Frederick Lessore.
Morning Post; *Referee*; *Daily Mirror*; *Daily Herald*; *Daily Sketch*; *The Star*; *Weekly Sketch*; *Country Life*; *The Sphere*; *Birmingham Post*; *Edinburgh Evening Dispatch*; *Glasgow Herald*;

Glasgow Evening News; *Gloucester Echo*; *Hull Daily Mail*; *Middlesex Chronicle*; *Western Morning News*.

Montreal Gazette.

1945 *The Hippodrome*, Spring Number.

1951 September. Beaux Arts Gallery II. Foreword by Frederick Lessore. *The Times*; *East Anglian Daily Times*; *Art News and Review* (John Blois).

1955 November. Wildenstein (shared exhibition).
The Times.

1972 June. Somerville Gallery I.
Arts Review (Webber); *East Anglian Daily Times*.

1974 June. Somerville Gallery II.
East Anglian Daily Times (Michael Webber).

1975 December 27. *East Anglian Daily Times* (Freda Constable).

1977 June. Aldeburgh Festival exhibition I. Foreword by Eric Sandon.
Festival Programme Book: Rosemary Somerville.

1985 July. Norwich Castle Museum exhibition. Foreword by Norma Watt.
Eastern Daily Press; *Norwich Mercury*; *Eastern Evening News*; *East Anglian Daily Times*.
Arts Review: Marjorie Allthorpe-Guyton (17 January 1986).

1986 February. Gainsborough's House, Sudbury, exhibition.
East Anglian Daily Times; *Ipswich Evening Star*.
Harpers & Queen: Jillian Powell.

1990 April. *Telegraph Magazine*: Joanna Laidlaw.
May. *The Child Art of Peggy Somerville* by Stephen Reiss, foreword by Hugh Casson. Pub. Herbert Press, London.
May. *A Broad Canvas* by Ian Collins. Pub. Parke Sutton, Norwich: includes a section on Peggy Somerville.

1991 June. David Messum Gallery I. Foreword by Stephen Reiss.
Eastern Daily Press. East Anglian Daily Times.

1993 April. David Messum Gallery II. Foreword by Stephen Reiss.

1994 May. *You Magazine* : Leslie Geddes Brown.
June. Aldeburgh Festival exhibition II. Foreword by Stephen Reiss.
Festival Programme Book: Ian Collins.
East Anglian Daily Times .
December. David Messum Gallery III. Foreword by Stephen Reiss.

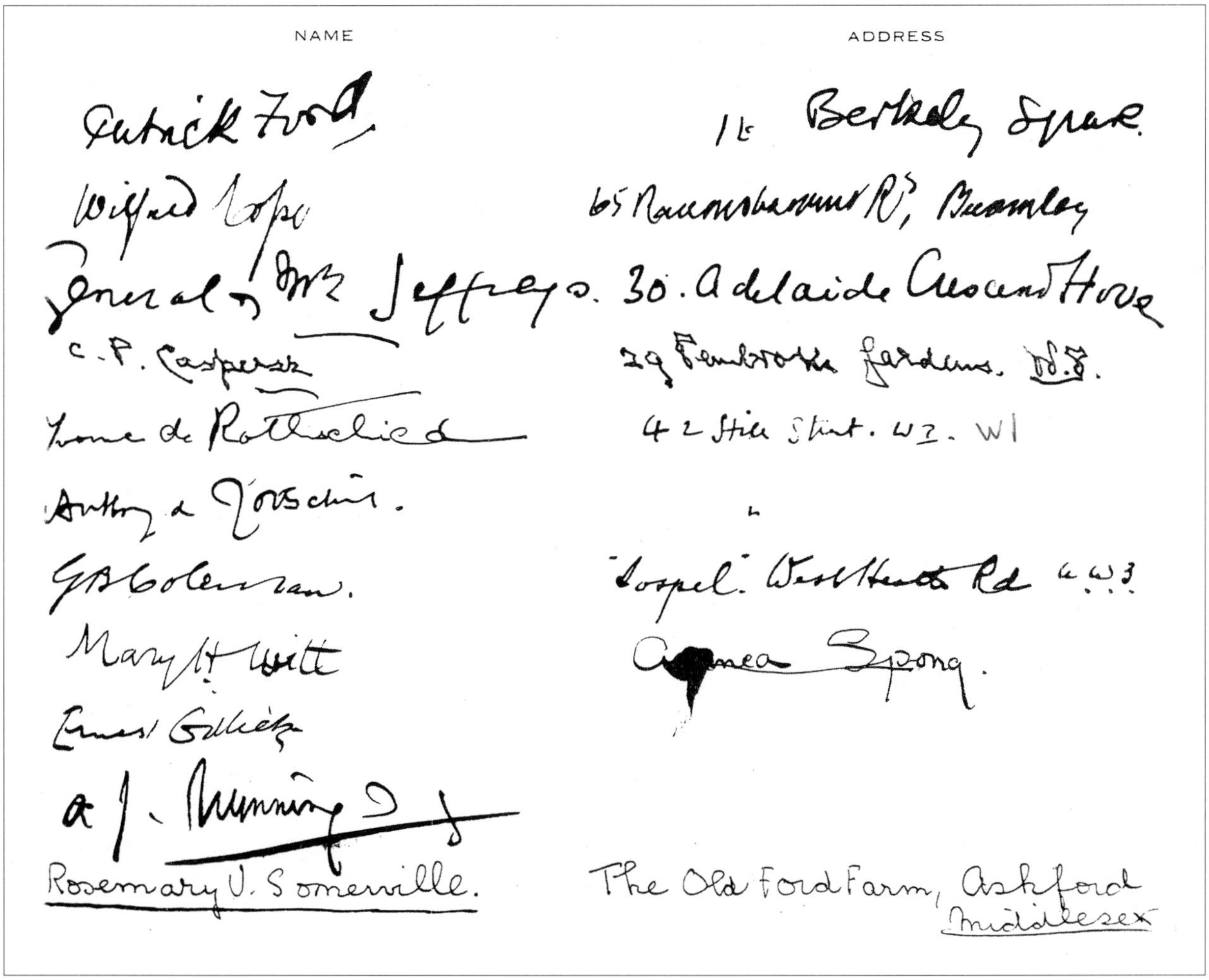

NAME — ADDRESS

Patrick Ford — 16 Berkeley Square

General & Mrs Jeffreys. — 30. Adelaide Crescent Hove

C. P. Caspersz — 29 Pembroke Gardens W.8.

Anthony de Rothschild.

G. B. Coleman.

Mary H. Witt

A. J. Munnings

Rosemary V. Somerville. — The Old Ford Farm, Ashford Middlesex

A page from the visitors' book for Peggy's first London exhibition in 1928. Visitors included A.J.Munnings, future President of the Royal Academy, and the Rothschild family who were among the buyers.

LUCY LOPEARS: A LUCKY ESCAPE.

Composed by Peggy in 1953 for the three daughters of her brother Forbes.

I am a Rabbit. My name is Lucy Lopears –
I live in a sandy bank sheltered by brambles in ~~fr~~
Nettle Meadow. Two wrens live in the ivy outside my
house and sing to me –

One ~~sunny~~ afternoon I was sitting in the ditch outside the back door.. The three of us were enjoying a quiet talk. The sun fell through the hedge and warmed my back.

We heard a dog bark at the farm. It was an excited bark I did not like – The wrens said they would go & investigate & flew off. I sat still, & almost fell asleep.... They came back with ~~alarming~~ the news that made me jump. This is what they had seen –

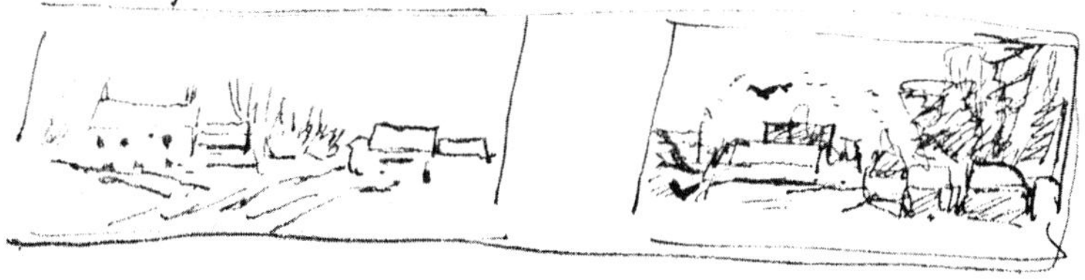

The Man had a spade for digging out rabbits and the dog
Then there were three little girls with fair hair –
was at his heels x They came straight to the Nettle meadow. If only
they had known how happy I was without them. I bolted through
my back door
Of course they went straight to my front door. The dog did not
even knock – His ~~nose~~ snorted down the passages with alarming
ferocity. But he was too fat to squeeze in – He scratched & whelped
Then I heard digging far above my head – I lay trembling, with my
eyes closed tight

~~The Noise seemed to~~ Grew ~~grow~~ louder
After a sound of ~~talking outside the back door~~
all seemed quiet then so I ventured to the B door
look out & this is what I saw –

Three little girls with fair hair
and the biggest one was looking straight
at me with ~~big~~ round brown eyes –
I believe she was as surprised as I was – I
popped back down and waited again.

~~The~~ My beautiful brown tunnel home was ~~becoming~~ very
collapsing. The Man & the dog were busy, with mountains of brown
earth around them. I heard the man shout ~~to Put you to pant~~ a
Block up the bolt hole – A tiny voice answered –

Suddenly ...

I saw a big spade

Coming straight down into my midst –
I turned in a flash for the back door – I went straight
for it the soil falling around me the dog only just missing
me – I saw the light – ~~for the~~ I saw the little girls face
Her big eyes looking at me & I thought she smiled –
She had pulled her boot out of the way
my way, and I was gone past her
along the ditch, faster, faster, faster faster
to freedom – – – – –

Afterwards ~~I heard from~~ ~~from the~~ wrens told me ~~I had a narrow escape~~ –
They saw the people going home and two grey brown rabbits
hung lifeless from the long handled spade flung across the mans
shoulder – ~~They said~~ I asked if the little girl was there, the one
with the round brown eyes – yes they said three little girls –
But ~~she~~ I could still see one was the one I knew & loved – she saved my life.
I heard the little wild duck fly across with a cry from

The fields towards the pond by the Stackyard - A sign of cold weather we all knew - we must go in search of a new home - We were right, tomorrow the world was white with snow - I hoped the little girl was as warm as I in my sandy home - I turned a somersault for joy.

Index